*That Light, All at Once*

# That Light, All at Once
## Selected Poems

JEAN-PAUL DE DADELSEN

TRANSLATED FROM THE FRENCH BY MARILYN HACKER

YALE UNIVERSITY PRESS ■ NEW HAVEN & LONDON

A MARGELLOS
WORLD REPUBLIC OF LETTERS BOOK

# CONTENTS

# Jonah

# Red in the Fog

I discovered the work of Jean-Paul de Dadelsen through a poem by Hédi Kaddour in his collection *Jamais un ombre simple*. Kaddour's twenty-odd lines hint at Dadelsen's preoccupations and his fate: music, a recollected provincial landscape, "discordant" obscenity or scatology, and even more discordant cancer.

**Jean-Paul de Dadelsen**
That light, all at once, to spark the unsteady
Flight of swallows, the carp's
Bubbles, women's bodies.
Despite the big-assed clock, words
Should only measure the newest
Hours, but how to shelter yourself
From your own refrain? You had
To know, didn't you, even when rhyme
Ceased to be reason, twisting
The octaves between the organs,
The fundamental progression of the bass,
The indispensable journey, and then the villanelle,
The worthless bird in the hand which still brings
Two wolves out of the woods, the dissonant
Reference to your balls: all of it
In the county fair and the bizarre weather
And the seamless tunic, honestly.
I would be cleansed, he said, if I burst

In the wind like an old pumpkin. A bit
Of night added on for cancer
And decompression, for the chord
At last free of memory. There will always be
Enough to fill a dream and put something human
Into the acoustics, but music
Like children, is always
Growing toward separation.

(translation mine)

Numerous poems by Kaddour and his coeval Guy Goffette pay oblique trib-
ute to modern or contemporary writers whom even a French reading public
may not know. It was because I had read and translated Kaddour's poem that I
picked up a collection of Dadelsen's work I noticed on a bookshop's minuscule
poetry shelf, leafed through it, bought it, read it. As an Anglophone reader, I was
surprised that the collected poems of a writer dead almost fifty years before the
book's publication apparently merited only two brief introductions—a three-
and-a-half-page memoir of the author by his friend and contemporary, the poet
and novelist Henri Thomas, and a biographical note.

What I discovered on reading the poems: an expansive (and very masculine)
voice, but capable of modulating itself in dramatic monologue, not a genre
explored much by contemporary poets in French—besides Bach, we find King
Solomon, Lot's wife, aging provincial women (a sequence of them) mourning
the constrictions of their lives, a Hungarian resistant in the uprising of 1956, a
sestina, a sort of villanelle—and a strong shaping sense for stanzas uncommon
in most French vers libres.

I began to render the work in English almost immediately, convinced by its
hybrid energy, breadth of imagination, and audacity.

❀

Jean-Paul de Dadelsen was born in Strasbourg, Alsace, in 1913. His studies were in German literature, with a special interest in German Romanticism.

He served in the French army from 1938 to France's defeat in 1940: he was an interpreter and aided the commander of a tank regiment in Belgium in 1940 in a battle for which he received the Croix de Guerre. Demobilized after the defeat, he went back to teaching; an early marriage ended in divorce in 1941. He was appointed to teach German at the lycée in Oran in Algeria, where he met and became close friends with Albert Camus and his wife, Francine, and wrote articles for the literary journal Sud. But in 1942, he traveled clandestinely to England, where he enrolled in de Gaulle's Free French Army and trained as a parachutist. He was then shifted to the information bureau of the Provisional Government, perhaps his introduction to journalism. He married again, an Englishwoman, Barbara Windebank: their two daughters, Anne and Alice, were born in 1944 and 1946.

He returned in secret to Paris in 1944, to the Ministry of Information of the Free French, and was posted to Berlin after the liberation, but chose instead to become a writer for Albert Camus's journal *Combat*. Soon after the war, he met François Duchêne, who was to be a lifelong friend, and with whom he shared the belief that a European Union would make future conflicts impossible. Duchêne introduced Dadelsen to Jean Monnet, former adjunct secretary of the League of Nations, who was to be one of the founders of the European Economic Union and, in 1968, the European Common Market.

Dadelsen worked at this time on the first draft of what was to become the "Opening Invocation" to "Jonah," not completed until ten years later. In 1946 he returned to London with his family to work as a correspondent for *Combat* and as a radio journalist for the BBC French Service. He was to earn his living as a journalist for what remained of his life. He wrote and broadcast a weekly French language radio "chronicle" every Friday on the BBC from 1946 until 1951: in France many people had kept the habit of listening to the "news from London" as they had done when it was clandestine during the war and the occupation, and it was listened to avidly on both sides of the Channel.

Henri Thomas recounts Dadelsen's years working at the BBC French Service after World War II. He was a wholehearted journalist who did not frequent literary editors, a man of expansive good humor whose life "had never been caught in the trap of being serious, whether as a teacher, a soldier, a journalist, even a public servant, which left him oddly free as he faced death." He describes his friend's penchant for tall tales and quixotic adventures, his clowning, and the unease that seemed to lie behind it. Neither Thomas nor Dadelsen's other colleagues had the slightest idea that he wrote poetry—although Thomas himself had published three poetry collections and two novels before the war ended. He writes of his astonishment upon reading "Bach in Autumn" in the *Nouvelle Revue Française* in 1955: "Nothing in what I knew of him prepared me for this, yet at the same time, how much it was him, how much that voice was his." And of how, soon afterward, Dadelsen gave him the manuscript of the sequence "Jonah," adding in an ironic note, "If you know what poetry is, hurry up and tell me."

The scripts of some of Dadelsen's broadcasts remain, on subjects as various as the meaning of the common and portentous phrase "Je vous aime"—in which he references Dorothy Strachey's classic *Olivia*—to his chronicle of November 11, 1950, a text titled "Ombre" (Shadow), which was part of his ongoing, solitary work toward the "Opening Invocation" ("Aux ombres: Invocation liminaire") of the symphonic sequence "Jonah," about his wartime comrades and their fates.

Dadelsen's English was formidable. His only efforts at poetry translation were, as far as I know, translations into French of a poet who wrote in Alsatian dialect, Nathan Katz. But probably in 1954, he wrote two long poems in English, "Stone in Vence," and "Prospect of Pisa": the former, a kind of elegy for his English mother-in-law, about the Roman graves in that town in the Alpes-Maritimes, and the latter a satirical multi-vocal piece starting with the set and characters of *Much Ado About Nothing*, including a limerick and a gentle jab at Stephen Spender and W. H. Auden: the British literary scene was also known to him.

Between 1947 and 1950, as a journalist and chronicler, Dadelsen traveled to Chile, attended international conferences in Berlin, Moscow, and Strasbourg, and was able to introduce his former schoolmate Georges Pompidou, future president of the republic, to General de Gaulle.

In January 1957, he went to New York for the first time, for the International Press Institute's annual conference. He had translated the American jurist Learned Hand's *The Spirit of Liberty* into French, and he met Hand during this trip. In Washington, he had a long meeting with the poet and diplomat Saint-John Perse, who had been living in exile in the United States since 1940. Dadelsen had fantasies of and hopes for a European Union, nourished by his friendships with Duchêne and Monnet, and perhaps it was meeting Perse that helped him crystallize these ideas into an essay, written early in 1957, on the possibility of a united Europe, an Afro-Brazilian federation, and hopeful alliances, some more historically plausible than others . . . even as, he was very much aware, the Hungarian uprising had met bloody repression while the rest of the world looked away.

During his trip to New York, he sprained his ankle, and he fainted on the flight back. From then on, his health deteriorated rapidly. Various specialists were unable to come up with a specific diagnosis. It was the local Zurich doctor who thought it might be a brain tumor.

Knowing he could have a fatal disease, Dadelsen began to make sure that copies of his—almost all unpublished—poems were in the hands of his friends.

In fact, though, it was his widow, Barbara, who worked toward and made sure of their posthumous publication.

He had surgery on March 19, 1957. He was admitted to the private Hirslanden clinic on May 7, with more affluent friends of the Dadelsen couple paying the fees. He developed pneumonia and died at the clinic on June 22. He was forty-three years old. His mother had died of bone cancer two years earlier.

Dadelsen had written poetry as an adolescent, and even theorized on it in letters to his uncle Eric, only seventeen years his senior, when he was in his late teens. But he had abandoned poetry until he resumed writing seriously in his thirties, after the war. His first published poetic work, the sequence "Bach in Autumn," appeared in the *Nouvelle Revue Française* in 1955, submitted by a friend, very likely Camus, to the editor, Jean Paulhan. It is a dramatic monologue in seven parts by a writer for whom the landscape around Leipzig and the timeless habits of its inhabitants were as easily familiar as the workings of an organ, the order of composition of Bach's masterworks—or a reading of Bible stories, so much a part of Alsatian Protestant worship.

Other poems, including the "Opening Invocation" to the Jonah sequence and "The Last Night of the Pharmacist's Wife," were published in journals during the following two years. Almost all Dadelsen's mature work, or what we have of it, was written between 1952, his thirty-ninth year, and the months preceding his death five years later.

After its publication, Dadelsen himself railed against the general admiration of "Bach in Autumn," which he thought was considered more "acceptable" than poems of his that were ribald and libertine, or more politically incensed and bleak, looking back on the toll the war had taken even on survivors, or simply lighthearted and iconoclastic. To my knowledge, though, the majority of these other poems would have been seen only by friends and perhaps a few literary patrons.

Most of his work appeared posthumously. The collection entitled *Jonah* was published in 1962, edited by Dadelsen's friend François Duchêne, with a preface by Henri Thomas. *Goethe en Alsace,* another collection of poems and essays, accompanied by reflections on Dadelsen by his contemporaries, was published in 1982; it included the powerful "The Bridges of Budapest," written six months before his death. His complete poems (excepting juvenilia) were published in the Poésie Gallimard series, in 2005: this and the hard-to-find *Goethe en Alsace* are the only editions of his poems now in print in French.

Dadelsen's bilingual Alsatian culture, its landscape, and his predilection for finding the earthy and popular sources in every art, or that of the artists he admired, are manifest in many of his poems. Though the poem "The End of the Day" (written in 1954) ventures as far as the Hermitage Museum in Saint Petersburg, it is to find there a Rembrandt that brings the poem back to the earth tones of Alsace's old Jews, Russian peasant exiles, the old man who comments—in German—on Colette's knowing human nature from the arse up, and Beethoven in old age, for whom a Stradivarius is one more garish cigar box. Why, then, with all this human communion, does the poem end in despair?

> Eternal One, you have broken us. Where now
> are outside, inside? Eternal One, you have
> broken us.

Dadelsen's portrayal of women in his poems is often that of a libertine, a satirist, or a frustrated lover. All the more surprising is the quiet and disquieting eloquent chorus of "Women of the Plain," a fugal series of dramatic mono-logues on a single theme, in a single landscape—one later visitors to the scene of the poet's childhood could recognize. It was intended, I think, as a multiple elegy for the poet's mother. These poems were written in the fall of 1956; he himself died in early summer the following year. But as well as a meditation on impending death (something he would execute brilliantly and heartrendingly in his 1957 sequence of Easter meditations), these poems consider the constricting surroundings and constricted lives of their rural or semi-rural Alsatian women. Not peasants, the "pharmacist's wife" and "tax collector's wife" are just educated enough to have read books with other horizons, listened to or played classical music, as they now wait for a husband, son, daughter to return from a distant horizon, bound to but not implicated in the sowings and harvests. They pray to a local saint like a crossroad demigoddess: even organized Christianity seems part of the too-distant wider world.

> Odile, you who were blind and not beloved,
>     pray for us also, women, still young,
> in the villages of the plain. The days are long,
>     the winter is long, the year is long, and so many long
> and empty years make such a short life!

Symphonic rather than fugal, the "Jonah" sequence, when published post-humously as a whole in 1962, confirmed Dadelsen's reputation (among the few who paid attention) as a major poet. It is a poem about war, composed after the war, addressing the shadow of war and the shadows of those the war took with it. It is an elegy for five comrades—one a painter, one a doctor—who died in combat, or who died afterward, destroyed by the experience: it is a shock to learn that Maurice, the painter, who was Jewish, later committed suicide by gas. Yet while the poem's first section demonstrates how war destroys, it also defiantly declares the love, neither sexual nor purely fraternal, between combatants. Their struggle seems self-contained: the occupation of France, deportations, and genocide are outside the poem's vantage point. The focus is on what the men lived and did or did not survive. In the sequence's succeeding sections, the tone changes, and Dadelsen the disabused observer emerges: the "whale" that swallows Jonah is society, conformity, organized religion—or its equally unsatisfactory absence. The sequence as published terminates with a long, polyglot, tragicomic tour de force, not translated here, about the poet's Alsatian Uncle Jean, who fought in the First World War.

The tone of the equally magisterial, and enraged, "The Bridges of Budapest" is different. It was written "in the valley of the shadow of death"—the poet's own death, and, preceding him, the violent demise of the short-lived Hungarian uprising of October–November 1956 against the Soviet-imposed government. Evidently written after the uprising had been suppressed, the poem is graphic and grotesque, tragic, if anything, in its absence of a tragic focus. There are no defeated heroes: we know nothing of the hanged men on the bridge parapets but their demise and decay. The preadolescent kamikazes seem premonitory now:

> little telegraph boys,
> a few girls thirteen, twelve, ten years old
> suddenly pubescent when it's a question of slipping, to strangle
>     him,
> into the butcher's alcove of metal and fire.

There is no evocation of "freedom" or any other principle: what we learn about the uprising is its macabre and rocambolesque conclusion: like a Bruegel or a Bosch, but closer up.

Dadelsen as a poet is much closer to Guillaume Apollinaire, the Apollinaire of *Alcools* and *Poèmes à Lou*, than to Stéphane Mallarmé. He is closer to Louis Aragon, too, but disabused of any idealism, political or erotic. Dadelsen was also a Germanist: in Alsace, this came naturally. He was a passionate reader of Heine, of Hölderlin, of Goethe, of Rilke. I wonder whether, after the war, he read Paul Celan or Nelly Sachs. But one can also see the influence of his English years and of T. S. Eliot—who is gently mocked in a poem ("It was Sunday . . ." ["C'était dimanche..."]) that itself has a somewhat Prufrockian stance—of Auden, and, it seems to me, of Louis MacNeice, who was probably a colleague at the BBC (at least, he worked there as a literary journalist during the same period). And Eliot himself is present in more than mockery. The poet Jacques Darras, himself an Anglicist and a translator, citing Dadelsen in a discussion of Apollinaire, made a connection, one I had thought of myself, between the work of Dadelsen and that of the Romanian-French Jewish poet Benjamin Fondane, who lived and wrote in Paris, and died at Auschwitz. Free of schools, cliques, and manifestoes, Dadelsen (like Fondane) draws on the poetic traditions of at least three languages, and writes as a man open to, and subjected to, history on the public and the private scale.

Dadelsen has been compared by at least two of his French contemporaries to Paul Claudel and Saint-John Perse, whom he clearly admired. But there is nothing like the personal, geographical and historical specificity of Dadelsen's poetry in their work, nor the storytelling, nor the use of demotic language. Even Dadelsen's (to my perception) Protestant references to biblical texts as stories— Lot's wife, Jacob and Rachel, King Solomon—quixotically true to his origins whether or not he remained a believer, is "alien" to most contemporary French poetry. For French poets who find this expansive specificity salutary—among others, Guy Goffette, Hédi Kaddour (who has since turned to the novel), Franck Venaille, Patrick Beurard-Valdoye, Jacques Darras, Marie Étienne, and Claude Ber—Dadelsen is, simply, a great modern poet. Less simply, he is one whose work links French poetry to at least two other traditions, German and English, a great poet of that European confederation, now the European Union, in which some of us now place as much hope, perhaps for less hopeful reasons, as he did.

*That Light, All at Once*

*Bach en Automne*

*Bach in Autumn*

## SUITE ALSACIENNE

Dans un noyer commode, à deux jets de pierre du village
qui se réveille à peine de sa somnolence hivernale,
un vol de corbeaux est posé, un sur chaque branche portante,
ils sont là, combien sont-ils, treize, dix-sept ?
comme de gros fruits noirs dans l'arbre dépouillé.
Est-ce le Consistoire de la confession d'Augsbourg
et ce gros-là, un peu sur le côté, est-ce le pasteur Schaeffer,
gros de cou, confortable de plumage, ayant épousé
une fille de pharmacien ou est-ce de médecin ?
Est-ce un comité ? Est-ce un conseil de clan, de guerre,
contre la buse qui toujours vole seule, et le faisan
mâle debout sur la route dans son plumage mordoré,
debout on dirait sur une patte avec sa fine queue pointue.

## ALSATIAN SUITE

In a convenient walnut tree, a stone's throw from the village,
barely awakened from its winter somnolence
a flock of crows has landed, one on each solid branch,
there they are, how many, thirteen, seventeen?
like big black fruit on the bare tree.
Is this the Consistory of the Augsburg Confession
that stout one there, is he Pastor Schaeffer,
with a fat neck, comfortable plumage, who married
a pharmacist's daughter, or was it a doctor's?
Is it a committee? Is it a family council, a council of war
against the buzzard always flying solo, and the male
pheasant who stands in the road in his bronze plumage,
standing you'd say on one foot, with his delicate pointed tail.

Sodome la sérieuse vantait ses finances, ses lois,
Et ni la guerre ni la prophétie n'avaient souillé la ville.
Sodome ménagère entretenait ses temples et ses toits.
Et dans sa fortitude apprise à ne pas implorer la pluie
Elle se gardait pure d'extases, de désordre et d'espérance.
Sodome étale avec intégrité ses remparts dans la plaine.

Je suis née dans un pays de rocs et d'eaux loin de la plaine
Dans un village goitreux de gens sans greniers et sans lois.
L'estropié tend un bol ébréché, l'idiot au sourire d'espérance
Chante et court sous la folle ondée qui contourne les villes.
La faim vient avec l'hiver, la fête après la pluie
Et parfois déguisé en somnambule Dieu marche sur nos toits.

L'ange apparut comme je languissais à la nuit sur le toit
Et vint me délivrer de la ville féroce des plaines.
Voici, je reviens vers ma patrie de pierre et de pluie.
Il m'a montré la porte secrète dans la muraille de leur loi.
Sur ce sentier déjà qui s'élève au-dessus de la ville
Je flaire sous le vent les espaces de l'espérance.

Ne te retourne pas. N'écoute pas. Laisse toute espérance
De sauver même cet enfant sourd-muet et ce chien. Les toits
Suintent sous la nue pourrie qui stagne sur la ville.

## LOT'S WIFE

Serious Sodom boasted its budgets, its laws,
For neither war nor prophecy had soiled the city.
Housewifely Sodom took care of its temples, its roofs.
With a fortitude earned by not praying for rain
And remained unsullied by ecstasy, riot and hope.
Honest Sodom spreads its ramparts across the plain.

I was born in a country of rocks and springs, far from the plain
In a goiterous village of folk with no silos, no laws.
The cripple extends his cracked bowl, the idiot, grinning in hope,
Sings and leaps under the wild downpour skirting the cities.
Hunger comes with winter; feast days follow rain,
And, disguised as a sleepwalker, God sometimes walks on the roofs.

The angel appeared as I languished one night on the roof
Who had come to save me from the savage city of the plain.
Now I return toward my homeland of stone and of rain.
He showed me the hidden door in the wall of their law.
On this path which rises above the city
I can smell on the wind the wide spaces of hope.

Don't turn back. Don't listen. Abandon all hope
Of rescuing even that deaf-mute child and that dog. The roofs
Seep beneath the foul cloud stagnating over the city.

Mais qui suis-je pour être sauvée seule parmi la plaine ?
Un âne brait. Un charretier et son cheval, ignorants de la loi,
Rentrent vers ce qu'ils croient une promesse de pluie.

Les arbres dorment sans rêves, depuis longtemps privés de pluie.
Les arbres dans la lumière qui baisse font des signes sans espérance,
Les chiens jouent. Une chatte fait ses petits. La loi
De son ignoble lave va recouvrir ces toits
Et ces fontaines qui vaguement chantonnent dans la plaine.
Que suis-je pour être sauvée contre la perte d'une ville ?

Seul Dieu, vrai Dieu, Dieu de toutes les villes
Dieu qui prodigue et qui refuse la pluie
Dieu qui jadis m'exila dans la plaine
Je ne veux pas survivre sans espérance.
Ces palmes sans malice, ces enfants sans amour, ces toits
Sans défense témoignent contre ta loi.

La femme de Loth, l'étrangère, regarde les toits
De tous ces hommes sans amour aveuglés dans la plaine
Et calmement descend se perdre dans la ville.

1953–54

But who am I to be saved alone on the plain?
An ass brays. A carter and his horse, knowing no law,
Return toward what they believe is a promise of rain.

The trees sleep dreamless, long deprived of rain.
The trees in the dimming light make signs without hope.
Dogs frolic. A cat gives birth. The law's
Base lava will wash over these roofs
And the fountains dimly humming on the plain.
Who am I to be saved in exchange for the loss of a city?

One God, true God, God of all the cities,
God who is prodigal with or who holds back rain,
God who exiled me long ago on the plain,
I do not want to survive without hope.
These harmless palm trees, unloved children, roofs
Undefended, all bear witness against your law.

Lot's wife, the foreigner, looks down at the roofs
Of all those loveless beings blinded on the plain
And, resigned, descends to be lost with the city.

# CRÉPUSCULE

Salomon sait la malice, la ruse, l'intrigue
la longue ambition dissimulée, la grande
concupiscence du pouvoir qui brûle les chétifs,
ceux qui jamais ne furent, jamais ne seront, rois.

Salomon a vu se ranger les armées, trépignantes
de sottise sacrifiée sous les torchons sacrés.
Salomon a connu, assis sur leurs sacs de laine,
les juges frileusement jouant à décider d'autrui.

Salomon n'est pas désarmé devant le soir
qui ouvrant le sérail laisse derrière la tenture entrebâillée
une longue lueur verte mourir sur les collines confuses
d'où un jour très lointain doit venir le salut.

L'heure n'est pas aux prêtres délirants, aux mages
prophètes sautants et glapissants de haine dédiée.
L'heure est tout entière, et pour des siècles encore, à la seule
attente d'une venue qui tardera longtemps sur les collines.

Il est des siècles où le temps stagne. Pourtant
belles les moissons, pleines les brebis, à flots
les génisses au soir, les femmes à foison
à grands frais amenées entravées de soie.

## NIGHTFALL

Solomon knows spite, subterfuge, intrigue,
tenacious hidden ambition, the overwhelming
lust for power that burns the puny
who never were, never will be, kings.

Solomon saw armies line up, feet stamping,
stupidity sacrificed beneath the sacred flapping rags.
Solomon knew the judges, seated on sacks
of wool, who cautiously played at deciding for others.

Solomon is not helpless facing the evening
that opens the seraglio, leaves beyond parted curtains
a long green light that dies on the muddled hills
from where, one far off day, salvation is to come.

This is not the time for delirious priests, for magi,
prophets leaping and yelping with dedicated hatred.
The hour is entirely, and for eons, only expectation
of an arrival that lingers a long time on the hills.

Time has stagnated for centuries. And yet
the harvests are abundant, the ewes fertile, the heifers
in the evening full of milk, the women plentiful,
brought at great expense, hobbled in silks.

Il est des nuits à se créer le vide dans l'âme
qui plane haut au-dessus du corps contenté
vide de toute brûlure. Il est des nuits où la chouette
crie sans désir et sans regret dans l'arbre mort.

10/8/56

There are nights that create an emptiness in the soul
as it glides above the contented body
emptied of all burning. There are nights when the owl
cries with no desire, no regret, in the dead tree.

Autour de nos reins les parois de la nuit sont rondes et sonores.
Dans la rumeur des artères heureuses et du sang contenté le cœur
Écoute s'ouvrir l'espace intérieur.

Les yeux fermés, regarde, telle une image dans une eau sombre,
À l'inverse de la fuite des mondes tournoyer des constellations obscures
Sous les voûtes de notre sang.
Les ténèbres du temple charnel sont vastes comme les profondeurs des cieux.

Noire, silencieuse, sourde jumelle du ciel visible, sœur de Rigel,
Sous nos paupières fermées écoute gonfler les jardins intérieurs,
Femme, porte du temps !

La palme vers le ciel sucré darde ses fruits nocturnes.
À l'homme tendu vers sa perte ouvre tes grottes marines,
Fais perdre pied à ce nageur
Pour qu'il t'éclabousse des voies lactées de ta descendance.

Mais déjà le premier oiseau pépie sur la branche confuse.
Les monts lavés naissent du safran oriental.
Il va faire jour encore.

Voici l'heure de cette trêve furtive
Où ni le ciel ne clame vers nous ni la terre ne nous attire

## A SONG OF SOLOMON

Night's barriers are supple, sonorous around our loins.
In the murmur of glad arteries, contented blood, the heart
Listens to inner space opening.

With your eyes still closed, watch, like an image in clouded water,
While the planets flee the other way, those dark constellations swirling
Under the arches of our blood
The darkness of the body's temple is vast as the depths of the skies.

Black, silent, deaf twin of the visible sky, Rigel's sister,
Listen to the inner gardens swell beneath our closed eyelids,
Woman, time's doorway!

The palm tree thrusts its night fruits toward the sugared sky.
Open your ocean grottoes to the man tensed toward his ruin,
Make this swimmer lose his footing
And splatter you with your descendants' milky ways.

But the first bird is already chirping on his misty branch.
The mountains are born bathed from eastern saffron.
Soon it will be day.

Now is the hour of that secret truce
When heaven does not call us or earth entice us

Et dans l'arbre qui dort sans rêves
La brise distraitement chuchote le nom de la patrie spirituelle.

Tourne vers ton souverain condamné
Ton masque de poupée qui sourit. Ô seule forte et seule sage,
Ô seule école de la mort !

5/20–8/3/53

And in the dreamlessly sleeping tree
A distracted breeze whispers the name of the soul's country.

Turn toward your condemned sovereign
Your smiling doll's mask. O only strong and wise one,
O death's only school!

## LES VERGERS DE TOMBOUCTOU

**Notice explicative**

Deux mille et onze, ô temps où des palmes sans nombre
Bruissaient, ombrageant tomates et concombres
Autour de Tombouctou,
Et des arbres mentaux, plantés par les édiles
Proposaient des vergers aux studieuses sybilles
Et aux dormeurs itou !

❋

J'étais sorti de mon corps endormi,
J'étais debout sous l'arbre à songes
Près de la citerne à souvenirs.
Le gardien me rappela que la pêche est
Interdite en cette saison et qu'il faut laisser
Mûrir les songes.

❋

Bel arbre que j'ai planté, arbre à réponses,
J'ai regardé souvent à la brise spirituelle
Palpiter tes feuilles doubles, pareilles
À la feuille sombre et claire du tremble.

❋

Il n'est pas bon de trop longtemps sortir la nuit
Dénouer sa chevelure sensible sous l'arbre à paroles.

# THE ORCHARDS OF TIMBUKTU

**Explanatory Note**

Two thousand and eleven, when palm trees without number
Rustled, shading tomatoes and cucumbers
All around Timbuktu,
And mental trees, planted by the town council,
Offered orchards to every studious sibyl
And to sleepers too!

❀

I emerged from my sleeping body,
I was standing under the dream tree
Near the memory tank.
The watchman reminded me that it wasn't
Fishing season, and that reveries had to
Ripen.

❀

Handsome tree I planted, answer tree,
I've often watched a witty breeze
Flutter your doubled leaves that resemble
The dark and light leaves of the aspen.

❀

It's unwise to stay out too long at night
Letting down your sensitive hair under the word-tree.

On apprend trop de choses. À la longue cela fatigue
Le pouvoir d'ignorer le lendemain.

❁

Dormeuse,
Je garde loin de toi les esprits des morts futiles,
Les pensées des voyageurs distraits, les désirs des
Vieillards affligés d'incontinence mentale.
Dormeuse, viens
Me rejoindre sous l'arbre à rencontres.
Je te porterai sur l'onde verte de ma respiration.
Je te dénouerai dans la lumière jaune de mon repos.
Demain tu te réveilleras
Contente.

❁

Les petites âmes aiment l'arbre à mensonges,
Les petites âmes vont y sécher leurs petites larmes.
Par de petits émois les petites âmes ajournent
La saison de grandir.

❁

Passés trente ans ne plante plus d'arbre à miroirs,
Passés quarante, taille court l'arbre à gloire,
Passés cinquante, arrose l'arbre à silence,
Pour qu'un matin, descendant au verger,
Pleuvent sur toi les fleurs de la tranquillité.

You learn too many things. In the long run it diminishes
    The power to be indifferent to tomorrow.

❀

Sleeper,
I will keep the spirits of the futile dead far from you,
And the thoughts of distracted travelers, the desires
Of old men afflicted with mental incontinence.
Sleeper, come
And join me under the meeting tree.
I will carry you on the green wave of my breath.
I will unbind you in the yellow light of my rest.
Tomorrow you will awaken
Content.

❀

Small souls love the tree of lies,
Small souls go to it to dry their small tears.
With small excitements small souls postpone
    The growing season.

❀

Past thirty, don't plant any more mirror trees,
Past forty, prune back the fame tree,
Past fifty, water the tree of silence,
So that one morning, when you come to the orchard,
The flowers of tranquillity will rain down on you.

❁

Je t'ai attendue sous l'arbre à fidélité,
Je t'ai espérée sous l'arbre à mémoire.
Excuse-moi. J'étais bête. Ô douce, ô sage, je te
Retrouve enfin sous l'arbre du sommeil.

❁

Somnus le mal nommé, échappé du sommeil,
Au mépris du code des déplacements mentaux et sans provision
Promenait sous les arbres à poèmes
            Son âme indûment plaintive.
On le ramena fermement, il n'était que temps :
En son absence, son stylo somnoactif avait
Tracé au parolier électronique le programme d'une
Ode qui eût fait instantanément monter
Le graphique du vagabondage passionnel.
La courbe de l'irresponsabilité oscillatoire,
La statistique de la prophétie illicite.
Contravention de huit jours de sommeil de rigueur.

❁

Les vacances du poète sont accordées
Par dispense spéciale du collège des vieillards
À chaque poète ayant guéri sept cas de surdité mentale.
Le poète alors, ayant presque épuisé son capital,
Au-delà des limites va seul, sans nourriture, sans guide,
            S'asseoir sous l'arbre de la mélancolie.

❀

I waited for you under the fidelity tree,
I hoped for you under the memory tree.
Forgive me. I was stupid. O sweet, O wise one, I will
Find you again under the tree of sleep.

❀

Somnus the ill-named, who escaped from sleep,
Despite the mental traffic code and without provisions,
Was walking his unduly plaintive soul
      Under the poem tree.
He was brought back with a firm hand, it was high time:
During his absence his somnoactive pen had
Inscribed on the electronic songwriter the program of
An ode which had instantly driven up
The graph of passionate vagrancy,
The curve of oscillating irresponsibility,
The statistics of illicit prophecy.
His fine: eight days of obligatory sleep.

❀

Poetic leave will be granted
By special dispensation of the college of the ancients
To every poet having cured seven cases of mental deafness.
The poet, then, having almost exhausted his capital,
Will go alone beyond the boundaries, with no food, no guide
      To sit under the melancholy tree.

## BACH EN AUTOMNE

### I

Les Juifs ce soir, sous les tilleuls, près des remparts, en prenant soin
De ne pas dépasser la lieue sabbatique, promènent leurs chapeaux noirs.
Frères d'Élie et de Naboth, la paix soit avec vous !
Dernier des jours anciens, samedi s'étire au soleil qui s'éloigne.
C'est le jour où la terre, même sous la herse d'octobre, se souvient
D'avoir porté, dedans son ventre saturé de sucres funèbres,
            Le Corps du Fils de l'Homme.

Dans l'église à grande eau les femmes frottent les dalles. Tout à l'heure
Elles rentreront balayer devant leur porte et rempliront d'huile
            La lampe du septième jour.
Nous sommes nés pour porter le temps, non pour nous y soustraire,
Ainsi qu'un journalier qui ne quitte la vigne qu'à la tombée du soir.
Mais au seuil de la dernière nuit de notre semaine, il est doux d'écouter
            Dimanche en marche sous l'horizon.

Seul le noyer mûrit encore ses fruits tardifs, pareils à nos cerveaux.
Le vent qui parmi l'herbe et sur les eaux sème son gain de feuilles
            Bientôt nous ouvrira l'espace encore voilé.
À la fenêtre de ses nids caducs, l'hirondelle en tumulte
            Crie vers son autre pays. Bienvenus,
Soir de notre journée, samedi de notre vie, saison aux mains ouvertes !
            Seigneur, je suis content.

# BACH IN AUTUMN

## I

The Jews this evening, under the lindens, near the ramparts, taking care
Not to exceed the Sabbath mile, are promenading their black hats.
Brothers of Elijah and Nabaoth, peace be with you!
Last of the ancient days, Saturday stretches out in the distancing sun.
It's the day when the earth, even beneath October's harrow, recalls
That it once bore in its womb soaked with funereal sweetness
      The Body of the Son of Man.

In the church, women sluice down the tiles. Later
They will go home to sweep in front of their doorsteps and will fill with oil
      The lamp of the seventh day.
We are born to bear time, not to elude it,
Like a day laborer who only leaves the vineyard at nightfall.
But on the threshold of the last night of our week, it is sweet to hear
      Sunday moving across the horizon.

Only the walnut tree is still ripening its late fruit, like our brains.
The wind that scatters its hoard of leaves in the grass and on the waters
      Will soon open that still-veiled space to us.
At the windows of their outworn nests, a hubbub of swallows
      Cry out toward their other country. Welcome,
Dusk of our day, Saturday of our life, open-handed season!
      Lord, I am content.

## II

J'ai connu jadis les jours de marche, les ormes vers le soir énumérés
De borne à borne sous le soleil chromatique,
L'auberge à la nuit où fument quenelles de foie et cochon frais.
Jadis à libres journées j'ai marché jusqu'à Hambourg écouter le vieux maître.
Haendel en chaise de poste s'en est allé
Distraire le roi de Hanovre ; Scarlatti vagabonde dans les fêtes d'Espagne.
Ils sont heureux.

Mais à quoi serviraient les pédales des orgues, sinon
À signifier la route indispensable ?
Sur ce chemin de bois, usé comme un escalier, chaque jour, que ce fût
Sous les trompettes de Pâques ou les hautbois jumeaux de Noël,
Sous l'arc-en-ciel des voix d'anges et d'âmes,
De borne à borne répétant mon terrestre voyage, j'ai arpenté
La progression fondamentale de la basse.

Au-dessus de la route horizontale par où les négociants partent non sans péril
Marchander aux échoppes de Cracovie
Les perruques, les parfums, les peaux apportées des éventaires de Novgorod,
Seule l'alouette s'élance dans la verticale divine.
Avant qu'à Ia suite de son Soleil
Hors de la tombe, de l'ordre, de la loi, l'âme éployée ne parvienne à jaillir.
La terre apprise avec effort est nécessaire.

## II

Once I knew days spent walking, the elms numbered toward evening
>     From milestone to milestone beneath a chromatic sun;
At night the inn where liver dumplings and pork were steaming.
Then, on my free days I would walk all the way to Hamburg to hear the old master.
>     Handel has gone off in a post chaise
To amuse the king of Hannover; Scarlatti wanders through Spanish feast days.
>     They are happy.

But what use are the organ's pedals, if not
>     To mark the indispensable way?
On this wooden path, worn like a staircase, daily, whether
Under the Easter trumpets or the paired Christmas oboes,
>     Under the rainbow of heaven's and human voices
From milestone to milestone repeating my earthly voyage, I followed
>     The bass line's fundamental progression.

Above the horizontal road that merchants take, not without risk,
>     To bargain in the shops of Kracòw
For wigs, perfumes, pelts from the stalls of Novgorod,
A lark soars alone in the holy vertical.
>     Before the wingspread soul in its sun's wake
Can spring forth beyond the tomb, the rules, the law,
>     This earth must be learned the hard way.

## III

Lente, coupée de silences, progressant par frissons, la sarabande catalane
Se meut dans les espaces de la nuit. Selon qu'elle dresse ou
Creuse ses spirales, elle se hisse aux feux d'Aldébaran ou plonge au nadir
Dans le branchage haletant des artères traverser les amants réunis.
Les yeux clos sur le hennissement de leurs cœurs accordés, ils écoutent
Le sang obscur s'ébrouer vers leur mort en éclaboussures de vivaces étoiles.
       La chair est nécessaire.

Le rude Luther donna son avis sur ce point. Jacob désira Rachel
Deux fois sept années. L'homme, afin de perpétuer sa vigueur
Et la longue impatience de sa lignée, les confie à cette compagne, complice
De la terre, et comme elle savante, sournoise, habitée d'eaux infatigables,
Gorgée d'acides plus durables que nous. Rien ne survit seul. En des méandres
Incalculables le corps de Rachel prépare la Pâque de notre espèce.
       Tout n'est pas raisonnable.

Je connais l' attirance de la nuit. La gamme la plus tendue retrouve
Pour descendre à ces vibrations pourpres une pente irrésistible.
Peut-être le désir n'est-il que le déguisement d'une nostalgie de l'âme
Effrayée dans l'obscurité ? Au pied des échelles du songe,
Repoussant l'ange, fermant les yeux, Jacob de tous ses reins vautré
En gémissant étreint la vraie terre, la vraie mort. Bételgeuse au zénith
       Tremble aussi au fond des puits.

Comme, vers la maison de sa jeunesse, l'Enfant prodigue, le plus fidèle,
Ainsi, dans le monde en travail prenant sa part, l'âme voulut peut-être

## III

Slow, sliced by silences, progressing in shivers, the Catalan sarabande
Moves through night's interstices. As it flings up or
Hollows out its spirals, it hoists itself to Aldebaran's flames or dives to the depths
Of the arteries' panting branches across the reunited lovers.
Their eyes closed on their tuned hearts' whinnying, they hear
Their dark blood as it shudders toward death in bright star splashes.
      The flesh is necessary.

Harsh Luther told his thoughts on this. Jacob desired Rachel
Two times seven years. A man, to perpetuate his strength
And the long impatience of his lineage, entrusts them to this companion, earth's
Accomplice, and, like earth, knowing, sly, inhabited by tireless waters,
Imbued with acids that outlast us. Nothing survives alone. In its incalculable
Detours, Rachel's body prepares our species' Easter.
      Not everything is reasonable.

I know night's attraction. The tautest scale will find
An irresistible slope plunging to those crimson vibrations.
Perhaps desire is only a disguise for the soul's nostalgia,
Afraid of the dark? At the foot of the ladder of dream,
Pushing the angel away, closing his eyes, Jacob sprawls on
His loins, moaning, clasps true earth, true death. Betelgeuse too at its zenith
      Shivers in the depths of the well.

Like the Prodigal Son, the one most faithful to the home of his youth,
As it takes its part in the laboring world, perhaps the soul wishes

Renaître les yeux bandés, loin du jour, et refaire à tâtons
Le chemin vers la lumière natale. L'heure viendra où le Père
Ouvrira les portes de la pesanteur. Passé le dernier combat, franchis
Les derniers feux, l'âme se dénouera dans les échos sans fin
        D'un accord sans mémoire.


**IV**

Le ciel au soir est vert. À la lisière du bois les chevreuils
Viennent humer au loin les villages roux de feuilles et de fumées.
Bientôt, quand avec la nuit tombera le vent de Pologne,
        La brume montera des prés.

Le regard du faon découvre trois lieues de plaine sans refuges.
Autour du sommeil des hameaux les barrières vermoulues n'arrêtent
        Ni les reîtres ni la peste.

Le monde dans l'espace et la durée étale sa placidité.
J'ai lu longtemps dans ce livre perpétuel. Autrefois j'ai décrit
Les gambades au mois de mai du jeune agneau,
        Le vol instable des émouchets.

Je ne décrirai plus. Tout est nombre. L'arbre,
Rivière de feuilles ou noir de gel, entre la terre et le ciel instaure
        Une figure permanente.

Le monde est en repos, dit-on ; les princes sont en paix, peut-être.
Entre la nue basse et l'horizon convexe s'éloigne une gloire exténuée

To be reborn blindfolded, far from day, and grope its way back
Along the path toward birthlight. The hour will come when the Father
Opens the doors of gravity. The last combat over, the last fires
Crossed, the soul amid infinite echoes will set itself free
        In an unimagined chord.


**IV**

At dusk the sky is green. At the edge of the woods, roe deer
Come to sniff from afar the villages red with leaves and smoke.
Soon, when the wind from Poland falls with night,
        Mist will rise from the fields.

The fawn's gaze finds three leagues of plain with no shelter.
No end to the worm-eaten fences around the hamlets' slumber,
        No end to thugs and plague.

The world spreads out its calm through space and time.
I've read this never-ending book for long years. Once I described
The Maytime gambols of the spring lamb,
        The sparrowhawk's wavering flight.

No more description. All is number. The tree,
River of leaves or frost-black between earth and sky, imposes
        A lasting figure.

The world is at rest, they say; its princes are at peace, perhaps.
Between the low clouds and the convex horizon an exhausted glory

De lumière inaccessible. Le monde à travers fastes et largesses demeure
     Etabli dans l'exil.

Il faut rentrer. L'haleine de la nuit descend sur nos visages aveugles.
L'âme écoute approcher tes pas ; entre chez nous, Seigneur ;
     Il se fait tard.


**V**

À travers la futaie de l'orgue le souffle qui chantera la gloire du Seigneur
Est à larges semelles boueuses pompé par le fossoyeur sacristain.
Dans son effort boiteux sur le soufflet, le bonhomme, tête levée,
Bras à la barre, les jambes écartées, figure une difforme
     Étoile pentagonale.

À mi-chemin entre l'origine et la perfection des temps,
Cinq est le chiffre de l'homme, irrésolu parmi les choses certaines,
Désordre essentiel dans la balance du monde. Arbre mobile,
Animal hésitant, ange aveuglé, Adam dresse dans la lumière
     Le cri de son infirmité.

Le pâtre, le pêcheur, et l'arbre même sont minuscules sur la plaine.
Grand arbre horizontal, j'ai souvent regardé le fleuve. Ô platitude divine !
Tandis que sur un même obstacle l'eau successive répète une forme perpétuelle
L'Elbe depuis la mer jusqu'à ses mille sources demeure
     Partout présente d'un seul tenant.

J'ai vu l'oiseau judicieux pêcher de son bec courbe et jaune,
Le soleil d'entre les nuages allumer les bulles de la carpe. Ce sont

Of unreachable light moves away. The world with its pomp and its gifts
      Remains in exile.

Time to go back. Night's breath descends on our blind faces.
The soul hears your steps growing closer; come into our home, Lord;
      It's getting late.

## V

Through the thicket of organ pipes, the breath chanting God's glory
Is pumped by the thick muddy soles of the ditchdigger-sexton.
In his clumsy efforts on the bellows, the fellow, with his head raised,
Arms on the bar, legs spread, forms a misshapen
      Pentagonal star.

Midway between time's origin and its perfection,
Five is the human cipher, unresolved among things that are certain,
Disorder essential to the world's balance. Moving tree,
Hesitant animal, blind angel, Adam lifts in the light
      The cry of his weakness.

The shepherd, the fisherman, even the tree are tiny on the plain.
I often watched the river, great horizontal tree. O holy flatness!
Over the same obstacle successive waters repeat one perpetual form,
While from the sea to its thousand sources the Elbe remains
      Omnipresent, uninterrupted.

I have seen the judicious bird fishing with his yellow curved beak,
The sun between clouds glimmering on the carp's air bubbles. These are

Détails heureux. Mais gonflé de pluie ou rumeur dans la brume
La voix qu'impose le fleuve surgit de la constance
      D'une eau sans visage et sans nom.

Maintenant que ma vie est étale dans la plaine assombrie
Et que la nuit avec indifférence vient lisser mes eaux taciturnes,
Accorder-moi, Seigneur, à l'heure où de tes profondeurs
Affleure l'ordre sonnant des astres, de refléter encore
      Leurs intervalles immuables.

## VI

*Sur le nom de Bach*
(Dans la notation allemande, B = *si* bémol ; A = *la* ; C = *do* ; H = *si* naturel. Ainsi
traduit, le nom de Bach constitue un thème en *si* bémol mineur, qu'il a utilisé
comme troisième thème dans la grande fugue inachevée de l'*Art de la Fugue*.)

Dans la gamme couleur d'automne de si bémol mineur, descend
Cette première marche jusqu'à la note sensible ! Le nom alors se hisse
Jusqu'à do, le niveau de la réalité. Et, de nouveau, du même demi-ton,
      Retombe
Sur ce si dont la vibration suspendue appelle une nouvelle ascension.
Le clavier est l'image du monde. Comme l'échelle de Jacob
      Il nous traverse de bout en bout.

Regarde la corde tendue sur son frêle berceau de bois : chaque montée,
Même d'un dièze, augmente son effort. Mais pour descendre, simplement
      Relâche sa contrainte !

Happy details. But rain swollen or murmuring in fog
The voice the river imposes springs from the constancy
      Of faceless, nameless water.

Now that my life is becalmed on the darkened plain
And indifferent night comes to smooth my taciturn waters,
Let me, O Lord, at the hour when from your depths
The stars' resonant order surfaces, continue mirroring
      Their changeless intervals.

## VI

*On the Name of Bach*
(In German musical notation B natural is notated as an H, and thus the name Bach
constitutes a theme, used by Bach as the third theme of the great incomplete fugue in
*The Art of Fugue*)

On the autumn-colored scale of B-flat minor, descend
That first step to the leading note! Then the name raises itself
To C, the reality level. And once more, by a half-tone
      Drops down
To that B whose suspended vibration summons a new ascent.
The keyboard is the world's image. Like Jacob's ladder
      It goes through us from head to toe.

Look at the string stretched taut across its frail wooden cradle: each ascent
Even by one sharp, increases its effort. But to descend, it simply
      Loosens the tension!

Gamme qui s'élève avec peine, telle la femme de Loth, regardant en arrière, et
Sitôt qu'elle cède à sa pente, devient plus lasse encore, plus tendre aussi, plus
Condamnée, plus entraînée vers les eaux de l'amertume et de la séparation.
                    Que suis-je, livré à moi-même ?


Le renard pris au piège à dents aiguës se coupe une patte pour retrouver
Sa libre faim parmi les arbres noirs. La chenille se hâte vers le soir
Où elle ira se brûler à la lampe. Le cerf brame après la fraîcheur des eaux.
                    Rien n'est tout à fait muet.
Même la pierre est active. Rien ne se refuse, sauf,
Quand elle se complaît à elle-même dans les ténèbres de sa captivité,
                    L'âme.


## VII

*Sur le Très Saint Nom*
Sève dans les orgues végétales,
Chaleur par tierces aveugles dans les grottes du sang,
Lumière par quintes majeures mesurant le monde visible,
Esprit par inaudibles octaves exhalant, expulsant
À perte de pensée les nébuleuses d'âmes et d'anges,
Extérieur à toute chose, étranger à tout être
                    Dieu est.
Dans tous les êtres planté plus profond que leur identité.
Une activité sans partage habite la création partielle :
Lumière dans les racines de l'arbre, intelligence
Dans la migration gluante du hareng,
Feu dans les rocs, sève de l'âme,

The scale rises laboriously, like Lot's wife, looking back, and
As soon as it surrenders to the slope, becomes wearier, more tender also, and
Condemned, drawn more toward the waters of bitterness and separation.
      What am I, given over to myself?


The sharp-toothed fox caught in the snare gnaws off a paw to regain
His free hunger among the black trees. The caterpillar rushes toward the night
When she will fly into the lamp and burn. The stag bells for cool water.
      Nothing is entirely mute.
Even stone is active. The only thing that holds back,
Trying to make the best of it in dark captivity,
      Is the soul.


## VII

*On the Holy Name*
Sap in the vegetal organ pipes,
Heat in blind thirds in blood's grottoes,
Light in major fifths measuring the visible world,
Spirit's inaudible octaves exhaling, expelling
Till all thought is lost, the nebula of souls and angels,
Outside all things, foreign to every being
      Is God.
Within all beings, rooted more deeply than their selves.
An undivided movement inhabits partial creations:
Light in the tree's roots, intelligence
In the herring's slimy migration,
Fire in the rocks, the soul's sap,

Dieu indéfiniment déploie le monde
          Qu'Il nie.
Absent de tout lieu et d'une merveilleuse nullité de matière
Dieu n'est pas vie, vorace, vulnérable,
Volée à l'ordre minéral. Dieu n'est pas chaleur,
Vibration brève. Dieu n'est pas lumière, vaine
Semeuse de matière. Dieu n'est pas substance, fût-elle
Aussi vive, aussi volatile
          Que l'esprit.
Le monde qu'Il expire en une buée d'atomes,
Immensément petit infiniment fini le monde que Son haleine
Souffle dans l'espace factice et le temps saugrenu.
Une de Ses respirations l'anime, sans fin raisonnable,
Sans forme pensable, bulle dont les parois
Vertigineusement nous fuient ; une de Ses respirations
          L'annule.
          *

                  Mais au-dessous
Des êtres de flamme qui tournoient comme des soleils stagnants
Autour de Son insituable incandescence, au-dessous
Des séraphins, des chérubins, des trônes, au-dessous
Des vertus, des archanges, les anges messagers
Dans l'ombre appellent, atteignent, assaillent
          L'homme
Que leur regard traverse :
Au-dessous de notre amour de nous-même,
Au-dessous de nos idoles, nos vocables, nos pensées,
Au-dessous de notre peur et de notre demande, au-dessous

God continues to unfurl the world
    Which He denies.
Absent from all places, His matter wondrously null
God is not life, voracious, vulnerable,
Stolen from the mineral kingdom. God is not heat,
Brief vibration. God is not light, vain
Sower of matter. God is not substance, though it be
Lively and volatile
    As spirit.
The world He exhales in a mist of atoms,
Immensely tiny infinitely finite the world that His breath
Blows into false space and preposterous time.
One of His breaths brings it to life, with no reasonable end,
With no thinkable form, bubble whose surfaces
Flee giddily from us; one of His breaths
    Annuls it.

          \*

          But below
Beings of flame that turn like stagnant suns
Around His inscrutable incandescence, below
Cherubim and seraphim and thrones, below
Virtues, archangels, angelic messengers
In the shadows call, attain, assail
    Man
Whom their gaze goes right through:
Below our self-love,
Below our idols, our appellations, our thoughts,
Below our fear and our requests, below

De la voix qui me dit que je pense, que je suis, que je crois,
Au-dessous des étendues immémoriales de la patrie spirituelle
Au cœur de notre captivité secrètement le Seigneur se repose en Lui-même.

Du vide noir où perle une sueur d'hydrogène jusqu'aux semences
Cachées dans notre corps, des anges à l'amibe, l'énorme création
Est une seule chair sans partage, une tunique sans couture jetée
Sur quelle nudité, sur quel Corps effrayant de Dieu ?
Toute adoration charnelle est licite. Dieu dans les ténèbres de Noël
Nous demande, comme un enfant de notre fragilité,
       De le bercer.
Les anges de leurs sandales de lune parcourent les pays nocturnes,
De leurs ailes de silence couvrent le fugitif et la bête farouche des bois
—Ou les débusquent, pour leur perte souhaitable. Âme, ne crains point !
Comme le grain de blé, l'Éternel te tient dans Sa paume.
Il te jette au hasard de l'an. Il t'oublie sous la neige.
Il te lance en pâture aux oiseaux monstrueux de l'espace spirituel.
       Il te récolte.
          *

       Quelle âme ? Quel Éternel ?
      Belle âme en vérité, faite de vent et d'ordure !
Ô Sulamite, toute béante vers un Dieu qui te remplisse,
      Sultane affriolée d'un Dieu qui te choisisse,
Un Dieu tantôt satyre et tantôt pain d'épice ! On le connaît ton Dieu :
      Il s'appelle Nombril.
Qui, sinon Moi, adore le vrai Dieu dans Sa perfection première
      D'avant ce carnaval
De plan divin, de rédemption, d'amour offert ou refusé ?
      Âme, sœur de Rigel, voici l'heure

The voice that tells me I think, I am, I believe,
Below the immemorial expanse of spiritual homeland
At the heart of our captivity, the Lord rests secretly within Himself.

From the black void pearled with hydrogen sweat to the seed
Hidden in our bodies, from angels to amoebas, all of creation
Is one undivided flesh, a seamless tunic thrown
Over what nudity, over what terrifying Body of God?
All carnal adoration is licit. God in the Christmas darkness
Asks us, like a child of our fragility,
         To cradle him.
The angels in their moonlit sandals roam the nocturnal lands,
Shelter with wings of silence the fugitive and the wild beast of the forest
—Or flush them out, for their required end. Soul, fear not!
Like the grain of wheat, the Eternal holds you in the palm of His hand.
He tosses you randomly to the year's luck. He forgets you beneath the snow.
He throws you as food to the monstrous birds of spiritual space.
         He harvests you.

                              *

                 What soul? What Eternal One?
             A beautiful soul, in truth, made of wind and filth!
O Shulamite, gaping open toward a God who will fill you,
                 Sultana tempted by a God who may choose you,
A God sometimes satyr sometimes gingerbread! He's well known, your God,
                 He's called Navel.
Who, if not Myself, adores the true God in His first perfection
                 Predating this carnival
Of divine plan, of redemption, of love offered or refused?
         Soul, sister of Rigel, the hour has come

De rejoindre Abraham aux sphincters fatigués dont sortirent tant de rois,
De prêtres, de Messies ; voici l'heure
Ô fourmi de laboratoire, ô souris blanche, de repartir
Vers la douteuse issue des dédales simplets de
Dieu sait quelle expérience que tout à l'heure Il efface et
Recommence. Moi, je ne subis pas.
Moi seul pour le repos de tous travaille vers le jour
Où Dieu renaît à la perfection du Non-Être.

Ange de la mélancolie, que puis-je contre toi ?
Tu me connais mieux que moi-même.
Dans cette heure, la plus obscure, d'avant l'aube,
Que puis-je, aveugle et séparé,
Sinon, par mon vide même, mesurer encore
L'absence du Seigneur
Et, loin de mon été perdu, comme le chien d'Ulysse,
Écouter la nuit,
Écouter le vent, afin d'y reconnaître
Les pas de Son retour.

Dieu nous traverse
Comme la mer une méduse, d'un même mouvement qui tour à tour se gonfle
Et se creuse. Le tourbillon des galaxies est la phosphorescence de Sa vague.
Les myriades d'âmes sont un plancton flottant à Sa surface.
Il est la pente de notre sang vers l'estuaire de la mort. Il est
La marée de notre esprit. Il est notre orbite et notre folie.
Plus vaste que notre infini, plus ténu que l'atome, ce Je universel
Nous est plus intérieur que nous.

To join Abraham, from whose tired sphincters emerged so many kings,
      Priests, and Messiahs; the hour has come
O laboratory ant, O white mouse, to repair
      To the dubious exit from simplistic mazes of
God knows what experiment that He will soon enough destroy and
      Start over. As for me, I do not serve or suffer.
I alone for everyone's peace and quiet work toward the day
      When God is reborn to the perfection of Non-Being.

Angel of melancholy, how can I resist you?
      You know me better than I know myself.
In this hour, the darkest one before the dawn,
      What can I do, blind and apart,
But, by my very emptiness, measure once more
      The absence of the Lord
And, far from my lost summer, like Ulysses' dog,
      Listen to the night,
Listen to the wind, so I can hear
      His footsteps returning.

      God goes through us
As the sea through a jellyfish, in one movement that swells it
And shrinks it at once. The galaxies' whirling is the phosphorescence of His wave.
The hordes of souls are plankton floating on His surface.
He is the slope of our blood toward death's estuary. He is
The tide of our spirit. He is our orbit and our madness.
Vaster than our infinity, tinier than an atom, this universal I
      Is within us deeper than ourselves.

Qu'importe quand, comment, pourquoi nous fûmes roche ou reptile
Roi ou radis, Jacob ou Jonas ? Voici la rive du Jourdain !
Louons, au seuil du silence, ce corps qui nous fut prêté, ce temps, ce lieu,
Cette licence à nous donnée de proférer nos puériles louanges.
La chauve-souris aussi, et la taupe, et là-bas sur l'horizon épuisé
Cette maigre flamme de branches mortes honorent
       Le Nom indéchiffrable

                    Septembre 1952–Pâques 1955

What does it matter when, how, why we were rock or reptile,
King or cabbage, Jacob or Jonah? Here is the bank of the Jordan!
Praise, on the threshold of silence, this body lent to us, this time, this place,
This permission given us to offer up our puerile praise.
The bat, too, and the mole, and there on the exhausted horizon
That sparse flame of dead branches burning honor
> The inscrutable Name.

On te dira qu'après la pluie vient le beau temps ; on te dira
Qu'un tiens vaut mieux que deux tu l'auras.
     Ne le crois pas.
Il est bon qu'après la pluie vienne le déluge ; il est excellent
Qu'un tiens fasse sortir deux loups du bois ; il est nécessaire
Que pour ne pas aller assez souvent à la fontaine
     La cruche soit cassée.

Efface et recommence. On te dira qu'après deux 9 souvent vient le 36
Et qu'à Évian l'été dernier le zéro sortit trois fois de suite.
     C'est vrai.
Un colonel polytechnicien joua trois fois le maximum sur le zéro ;
Cent cinq mille francs ; merci pour les employés, merci monsieur pour les
Comptables du grand livre où sont inscrits depuis toujours vos
     États de service.

Campagnes sous Charles dit le Sage, sous Pyrrhus, sous Ramsès II,
Sous Hamourabi ; blessures neuf ; deux morts à l'échafaud,
     Un suicide,
Une vie ratée comme femme de magistrat. Comme décorations
Un enfant élevé contre tous, une parole tenue en dépit du bon sens,
Trois défaites par obstination contre l'évidence,
     Déshonneur et fidélité.

## THE GREAT LEDGER

They'll tell you that sunshine will follow the rain; they'll tell you
That a bird in the hand is worth two in the bush.
 Don't believe it.
It is good that after the rain comes the deluge; it is excellent
That a bird in the hand brings two wolves out of the bushes; it is necessary
That for not having gone often enough to the well
 The pitcher be broken.

Erase and start again. They'll tell you that after two nines there's often a thirty-six
And that last summer at Évian zero came up three times in a row.
 It's true.
A colonel who'd gone to the École Polytechique played the limit three times on zero;
Five hundred thousand francs; thank you from the employees, thank you Sir from
The accountants of the great ledger where your military service record has always
 Been noted down.

Campaigns under Charles known as the Wise, under Pyrrhus, under Ramses II,
Under Hammurabi; nine wounds; two dead on the scaffold,
 A suicide,
A life wasted as a magistrate's wife. As decorations
A child raised to despite everyone, a word kept despite common sense,
Three defeats by stubbornness against all evidence,
 Dishonor and fidelity.

Il lui dit : Et alors, tu es restée avec lui ? Eh bien oui, elle est
Restée avec lui, s'est fait sauter trois, dont la première fut
    Ratée pour elle
Et la troisième ratée par lui. Mais qui sait à quel titre
Cela faisait partie de son service à elle. Et de quel droit
Se serait-il senti si généreux, si magnanime, pour avoir pardonné ?
    Elle n'est à personne.

Je ne suis pas à moi. Je ne sais d'où je viens, je ne sais
Ce qui est marqué à mon compte ou contre moi
    Dans le grand livre.
Je ne suis pas mon oubli et ne suis pas ma paresse et ne suis pas
Ma pesanteur. Mais j'ai honte du plus profond de ma mémoire
J'ai honte de n'avoir pas crié contre toi
    Éternel.

L'Éternel est en moi qui me regarde moi, plus futile
Qu'un souffle de brise au soir sur une eau calme
    Et sans mémoire.
Il regarde du plus intérieur de moi mes pensées, mes idoles,
Mon besoin puéril d'un Dieu qui ait un prénom,
Mon désir insensé d'une femme qui n'aime
    Que moi.

La femme est sage. Jamais elle n'aime qu'à travers nous, n'aime
Que l'imbécile, le porc et le poltron caché en nous, n'aime que
    Notre mort
Que nous contenons comme la prune son noyau. Jamais ne tient parole,

He said to her: So you stayed with him? Well, yes, she
Stayed with him, got laid three times, of which the first
        Was spoiled for her
And the third spoiled by him. But who knows exactly how
That was part of her own service record. And by what right
Did he feel himself so magnanimous, so generous, for having forgiven her?
        She belongs to no one.

I don't belong to myself. I don't know where I come from, I don't know
What is marked down in my favor or against me
        In the great account book.
I am not my forgetfulness I am not my laziness and am not
My sluggishness. But from the depths of my memory I am ashamed
I am ashamed I did not cry out against you
        Eternal One.

The Eternal is within me and watching me, more futile
Than a breeze's evening breath over water, calm
        And memoryless.
He watches from deepest within me my thoughts, my graven images,
My puerile need for a God who has a given name,
My demented desire for a woman who will love
        Only me.

Women are wise. They never love except through us, love
The idiot, the pig, and the coward hidden in us, love only
        Our death,
Which we hold as a plum holds its pit. Never keep their word,

Jamais n'est chose cadastrable, jamais n'amasse mousse, jamais
Ne récompense l'insensé qui prétend oublier qu'elle est
    En service.

La maquerelle qui sut que la politesse est une forme de la charité
Sera l'aïeule d'un romancier d'une rare
    Élévation de pensée.
Le sperme de Saint Louis chaque jour coule à flots
Dans les paillasses de Bourgogne et de Basse-Bretagne.
Rien n'a ni rime ni raison, rien n'est pour notre usage,
    Après nous le beau temps.

Never are surveyed or measured, gather no moss, never
Reward the fool who pretends to forget that they are
    Under orders.

The madam who knew that politeness is a form of charity
Will be the great-grandmother of a novelist with a rare
    Refinement of thought.
Each day Saint Louis's sperm flows like water
Into the whores of Burgundy and southern Brittany.
Nothing has rhyme or reason, nothing is for our use,
    After us comes the sunshine.

## AMÉRIQUE DU SUD, HAUTS-PLATEAUX, GUITARE

Les travaux qui ne sont pas faits, ils se feront plus tard.
La nuit rouvre en secret les portes d'un pays ancien.
Guitare, que la main gratte, que la paume légèrement
    frappe, que le doigt
        pince pour la faire brièvement gémir et
           se résigner.
    Guitare, profonde fontaine.
À l'homme qui y jette un caillou, elle répond
par l'onde toujours plus ample de la mélancolie.
La mélancolie n'est pas une plainte, mais un lieu.


    Ai-je dit
les gendarmes venus pour la réquisition, la banque de
crédit et d'investissement, l'argent perdu aux dés avec
les fils de chienne enculée de la Compagnie des Autobus,
le maïs brûlé, l'enfant mort ? Ai-je crié ? Imploré ?
    Je dis la nuit, je dis l'absence
même d'une brise dans les arbres qui dorment sans rêves,
differents en ceci de l'homme, je dis
la corde pincée, ce creux frappé de la paume,
ce gémissement arrêté, recouvert de silence,
et comme lorsque l'on plonge une épuisette dans la rivière
si profonde qu'elle coule sans bruit aucun,

## SOUTH AMERICA: HIGH PLATEAUS, GUITAR

The undone tasks, they'll be done later.
In secret, night reopens the doors of an ancient country.
Guitar, that the hand strums, that the palm lightly
     strikes, that the finger
        plucks to make it briefly moan and
           resign itself.
     Guitar, deep well.
To the man who throws a pebble in, it answers
with the always widening wave of melancholy.
Melancholy is not a complaint but a place.

     Did I say
the police who come for their bribes, the credit
and investment bank, the money lost throwing dice with
the whoring son-of-a-bitch from the bus company,
the cornfields burned, the dead child? Did I cry out? Beg?
     I say night, I say the absence
of even a breeze in the trees sleeping dreamlessly,
different in that from men, I say
the plucked string, that hollow slapped by the palm,
that moaning stopped, covered over by silence,
and just as when you plunge a net into a river
so deep that it flows making no sound whatsoever,

la guitare jusqu'au bord et même
à déborder en flots sourds, la guitare présentement
   remplie de nuit.

Janvier '55

the guitar to the brim and then
overflowing in muted waves, the guitar that is now
    filled up with night.

## PEUPLIERS ET TREMBLES

Peupliers et trembles. Dans la dernière clarté horizontale
     à cette heure où la feuille la plus haute, qui tout le jour
     était prise dans la rivière de brise invisible
          soudain se fige en un miel de silence.

Pourquoi toujours ai-je reconnu le soir ?
     Le soir n'arrête rien
     — si ce n'est ce court instant irrésolu où la terre,
     ayant cessé d'inspirer, retient son souffle
     avant sa longue expiration nocturne —
     et tout à l'heure la chasse sera ouverte de toute dent,
     de tout œil, de toute griffe contre tout poil, contre tout sang.

     L'Éternel
     est un grand hibou au plumage de silence.
     L'Éternel est une martre.
     L'Éternel tue l'Éternel et se nourrit de son propre sang.
     L'Éternel est ce qui n'a pas de sens,
     n'a point de lieu, de nom, de temps —

Peupliers, trembles du soir,
     que j'ai aimé ces feuilles à deux couleurs
     entraînées pâle et sombre dans le courant de l'ample rivière invisible !

## POPLARS AND ASPENS

Poplars and aspens. In the last horizontal clarity
    at this hour when the loftiest leaf, which all day long
    was caught in the stream of invisible breezes,
        suddenly congeals in a honey of silence.

Why have I always acknowledged nightfall?
    Nightfall changes nothing
    —unless it's that brief unresolved instant when earth,
    having ceased to inhale, holds its breath
    before its long nocturnal exhalation—
    and soon enough the hunt will be on, teeth bared
    eyes bared claws bared against bared fur, bared blood.

    The Almighty
    is a great owl feathered with silence.
    The Almighty is a marten.
    The Almighty kills the Almighty and feeds on his own blood.
    The Almighty is that which has no sense,
    no place, no name, no time—

Poplars, aspens of nightfall,
    how I loved those bicolored leaves
    pulled pale and dark into the current of the wide, invisible stream!

Tout à l'heure, la recherche de la chaleur, les grottes,
    les profondeurs de la nuit créée, la plongée
        vers les eaux souterraines, mais maintenant
    ce court arrêt, la largeur à peine d'un fuseau horaire,
        ailleurs meuglent les usines, les rotatives,
    ici même aux fenêtres de grands express européens
        la matrone hollandaise entre Colmar et Mulhouse regarde
Bolwiller tout éperdu dans un miel solennel.

Rien de réglé, rien de promis, le soir n'apporte rien.
    Ô confitures du quiétisme ! miel vénéneux à l'âme, et pourtant
        le soir est l'image du pays natal
    le soir nous ouvre un pays ancien.

Later, the search for warmth, the grottoes,
    the depths of created night, the dive
        into subterranean waters, but now
    this brief pause, barely as wide as a time zone,
        elsewhere factories bleat, and presses,
    here, even at the windows of the great European express trains
        between Colmar and Mulhouse, the Dutch matron looks out at
    Bollwiller drowned in ceremonious honey.

Nothing is settled, nothing promised, nightfall brings nothing.
    O jam pot of quietism! honey that poisons the soul, and yet
        nightfall has the face of a homeland
    nightfall opens an ancient country to us.

## LA FIN DU JOUR

Voici
dans la vitrine de comestibles fins
les noirs homards, les langoustes,
une antenne brisée, une patte arrachée,
l'œil un bouton de bottine très noir
très en colère
                — mais comment y aurait-il
colère où il n'y a aucun apitoiement sur soi ?
ni regret ? ni peur ? seulement
rupture, recherche encore,
la patte encore tâtant le sol obscur,
l'antenne qui cherche.

            Ainsi, parfois, les vieux :
trop courbés pour prétendre encore,
trop cassés pour mentir.

Comme
les vieilles femmes russes de l'exil
quand vient le pope, ancien cosaque,
tirent, de dessous le lit, un pot de confiture,

et comme
les très vieux juifs,

## THE END OF THE DAY

Here
in the shop window full of delicacies
the black lobsters, the langoustines,
a feeler broken, a claw torn off,
eye a deep black boot button
terribly angry
                    —but how could there be
anger with no self-pity?
or regret? or fear? only
rupture, still searching for
the claw still groping the dark surface
the feeler feeling.

          Thus, sometimes, the old:
too bowed down to keep pretending,
too broken to lie.

Like
the old Russian women exiles
when the pope, former Cossack, arrives
they pull a jam pot out from beneath the bed,

and like
the very old Jews,

regardant encore, au soleil qui ne réchauffe plus,
les tétons de la jeune bouchère kosher et myope,
ou, le soir à la cuisine, du petit-fils
debout dans la bassine d'eau tiède, les couilles où dort
la descendance de la douce et profonde Rachel,

et comme
le père R. K., crustacé de grand âge,
de grande saumure austro-morave,
le père K., un matin de neige, debout sur ses jambes mortes,
mettant ses bretelles et parlant de
Colette (alors morte depuis peu) :
«Ja, die kannte die Leute.
Die kennt die Leute : bis in den Arsch hinein. »

et comme
le vieux Ludwig, après tant de
sonates inutilement explosives,
s'amusant à présent
à fredonner pour lui seul, et peu lui importe
que le trait soit béatifique ou grinçant sur ces
vieilles boîtes à cigares de Stradivarius,
Guarnerius, Amati, Tutti Quanti, ce qui
l'intéresse, batifolage de baleine
bourrée de kermesses stellaires, ce qui
l'intéresse, c'est ce bout de chanson transfiguré et
l'espace autour, l'immobilité, la nuit autour de la
chanson filée droite et sans mentir,

who still watch, in the no longer warming sun,
the tits of the kosher butcher's nearsighted young wife,
or, in the kitchen at nightfall when the grandson
stands in a basin of lukewarm water, his balls
where sweet deep Rachel's descendants sleep,

and like
old R.K., ancient crustacean,
in ancient Austro-Moravian brine,
old R.K., one snowy morning, standing on his dead legs,
pulling up his suspenders, and talking about
Colette (just recently dead):
"Ja, die kannte die Leute.
Die kennt die Leute: bis in den Arsch hinein."

and like
old Ludwig, after so many
uselessly explosive sonatas,
now amusing himself
humming just to himself, and what did it matter
if the tune was heavenly or grating on those
old cigar boxes made by Stradivarius,
Guarnerius, Amati, tutti quanti, what
interests him, a whale dallying,
bourrées at stellar county fairs, what
interests him is that bit of transfigured song and
the space around it, immobility, night around the
song drawn straight out and with no lying,

ainsi, au soleil qui ne réchauffe plus, les vieux :
dans la carcasse rompue, un regard s'est ouvert.

Ainsi, à l'Ermitage
parmi tant de noblement Poussin sur qui
La Néva pose ses reflets de gel,
le vieil Hendrijk, désormais se foutant d'être
de bon ton ou baroque ou structuré, peignant
à truellées de terres épaisses, à traînées
de couleur grattées au fond des pots, peignant
cette haute chose rectangulaire et, tout à droite,
sans raison anecdotique la moindre, ce personnage
indispensablement vertical et
le dessous des
                    sandales de l'Enfant Prodigue et les
                    épaules courbées vers lui du Père.

Nous fûmes entiers, carapacés de noir et de dur.
Éternel, tu nous as rompus. Où est présentement
le dehors, le dedans ? Éternel, tu nous as
                    cassés.

1954

thus, in the no longer warming sun, the old:
in their broken carcasses, an opening gaze.

Thus, at the Hermitage
among so many nobly Poussin on whom
the Neva fixes its icy highlights,
old Hendrijk, henceforth not giving a fuck about being
tasteful or baroque or structured, painting
with trowels full of thick earth, with smears
of color scratched from pot bottoms, painting
that high rectangular thing, and, to the right,
without the slightest narrative reason, that character
indispensably vertical and
the soles of the
                Prodigal Son's sandals and the
                Father's shoulders bent toward him.

We were whole, black-carapaced and hard.
Eternal One, you have broken us. Where now
are outside, inside? Eternal One, you have
                broken us.

# EXERCICE POUR LE SOIR

Arrête-toi. Au lieu de haleter de seconde en seconde
Comme un torrent de roc en roc dévalant sans vertu,
Respire
Plus lentement et sans bouger, les pieds croisés, les mains jointes,
Regarde, comme si c'était le monde tout entier,
Un objet, menu et domestique, par exemple
Cette tasse.

Néglige sa courbure, ce bord ondulé, ces dessins bleus.
Ne considère que l'intérieur, cette cavité blanche, cette surface
Lisse.
L'eau n'est lisse ainsi que les soirs de grand calme
Après une journée qui rassemble et retient son bonheur
Au centre du silence où s'arrête son
Souffle.

Peux-tu nommer un jour, une heure, sans reflets d'hier,
Sans impatience de demain, où ton âme fut ainsi
Lisse ?
N'écoute pas ton cœur, ne compte pas ton pouls, ne songe pas
Au temps qui vers la mort te traverse, mais seulement
En arrêtant ton souffle regarde cette pure et seule qualité
De lisse.

## EXERCISE FOR THE EVENING

Stop. Instead of panting and gasping from second to second
Like a torrent hurtling from rock to rock with no special merit,
Breathe
More slowly, without moving, ankles crossed, hands clasped,
Observe, as if it were the whole world at once,
An object, slight and domestic, for example
This cup.

Ignore its curve, its undulating surface, this blue pattern.
Consider only the interior, this white cavity, this surface's
Smoothness.
Water is only smooth like this on evenings of exceptional calm
After a day which gathers and holds back its joy
At the center of the silence where its breath
Stops.

Can you cite a day, an hour, with no echo of yesterday,
No haste for tomorrow, when your soul was as
Smooth as this?
Don't listen to your heart, don't measure your pulse, don't envision
Time moving through you toward death, only
While holding your breath look at this pure and only quality
Of smoothness.

Si maintenant tu apprenais à fixer ton regard, ta pensée,
Ton âme sans ciller sur quelques centimètres carrés de
Lisse,
Peut-être alors, sans fuir le monde, sans éviter les femmes,
Sans changer d'état, de pays, de nourriture,
Pourrais-tu espérer un jour commencer à comprendre
Le monde entier.

C'est une tasse sans valeur achetée dans une épicerie-mercerie
D'un village savoyard du côté de Boège et Séchemouille.
Elle n'est pas lisse.
Le microscope y trahirait un Himalaya d'aspérités.
Ce qui la fait lisse, c'est la lumière, ce sont tes doigts naïfs.
Pour un autre regard, peut-être, une tasse
Vaut une tête.

Autant que l'orgue solennelle ou la machine électronique,
Autant que l'orage équatorial et les courants du Pacifique
Cette tasse
Honore le Nom divin. Si demain tu étais exilé, tu n'aurais pas
Besoin, à condition de l'avoir regardée longtemps, à condition
De pouvoir dans ton cœur recomposer ce lisse, d'emporter
Ce tesson.

Voici l'entrée, non pas de la sagesse, ni du silence,
Ni du parfait pouvoir sur toi-même et ton ombre,
Mais d'une première
Cavité assez lisse pour contenir une poignée de paix.

If you learned now to fix your gaze, your thought,
Your soul without blinking on a few square centimeters of
Smoothness,
Perhaps, without leaving the world or the company of women,
With no change in your health, your country, your diet,
You might aspire one day to begin to understand
The whole world.

It's a cup of no value, bought at a dry-goods and grocery shop
In a Savoyard village near Boëge and Séchemouille.
It isn't smooth.
A microscope would reveal Himalayas of cracks.
What makes it smooth is the light, is your ingenuous fingers.
To a different gaze, perhaps, a cup is worth
A head.

As much as the solemn organ or the electronic machine,
As much as the equatorial storm or the Pacific tides
This cup
Honors the holy Name. If you were exiled tomorrow, you would not
Need, provided that you had looked at it long enough, provided
You were able to reconstruct this smoothness in your heart, to bring
This shard along.

Here is the entrance, not to wisdom, nor to silence,
Nor to perfect control of yourself and your shadow,
But to a first
Cavity smooth enough to hold a handful of peace.

Maintenant tu peux dormir, les pieds joints pour ne pas couper
Le courant, les mains jointes, maintenant tu peux
T'élever

Lentement, calmement un peu plus haut que ton corps étendu
Et dénoué, comme si tu n'habitais plus que ta tête
Ou tes narines
Ou les environs immédiats de l'œil pinéal ;
Maintenant au-dessus de ton corps pacifié, au-dessus
De ta boîte à sornettes, dans le fluide lisse de ton âme éployée, tu peux
Veiller.

Now you can sleep, your feet together so as not to break
The current, hands clasped, now you can
Rise

Slowly, calmly, a little higher than your body, recumbent
And loosed, as if you inhabited only your head
Or your nostrils
Or the immediate vicinity of the pineal gland;
Now, above your pacified body, above
Your box of balderdash, in the smooth fluid of your unfurled soul, you can
Keep watch.

# VARIATIONS SUR UN THÈME DE BAUDELAIRE

*«Mon enfant, ma sœur…»*

## 1

Inconnue, comme si je t'avais faite d'une femme étrangère,
Je te devine pourtant comme si nous sortions du même ventre.
Contre mon cou ton cœur plus jeune
Mesure une heure plus neuve que la mienne, ô confiante
Ennemie et douce complice au même instant, écoute
Nos sangs alliés s'emplir d'une même rumeur qui monte
Du fond de la nuit natale.

## 2

Par-delà les années où tu ne m'avais pas rejoint, par-delà
Les défenses des totems futiles, bien plus nouveaux que nous,
Je te retrouve.
Je devrais pouvoir te sourire enfin et par la main
Te mener vers l'époux d'une autre tribu. Ô dangereuse et secrète,
Je reconnais ton regard morose et patient qui me rappelle sans paroles
Que notre soif n'est pas étanchée.

## 3

Qui me prouve, silencieuse, que tu dis vrai ? Je ne
Vous connais pas, Madame, et n'aurai pas de quoi vous satisfaire.

# VARIATIONS ON A THEME OF BAUDELAIRE

*"Mon enfant, ma sœur . . ."*

## 1

Unknown, as if I had begotten you with a foreign woman,
I can understand you, though, as if we came from the same womb.
Against my neck your younger heart
Marks a newer hour than mine, O confident
Enemy and sweet accomplice all at once, listen
To our linked bloodstreams filling with the same murmur that rises
From the depths of our natal night.

## 2

Beyond the years where you did not come to join me, beyond
The useless totems' defenses, so much newer than we are,
I find you again.
I should be able to smile at you at last and take your hand
To lead you to the spouse from another tribe. O dangerous and secret one,
I recognize your sullen, patient look that wordlessly reminds me
Our thirst is not quenched.

## 3

Who will prove to me, silent one, that you are telling the truth? I do
Not know you, Madam, and do not have what would satisfy you.

Rentrez donc chez votre mari !

Je ne suis pas qui vous croyez. Nous nous montons le cou, belle dame !

Cette saison est traître, où tout travaille caché dans la terre.

Mais dis donc quelque chose ! parle ! pour démentir enfin cette implacable

Certitude de ton silence.


4

Les temples étaient neufs. On prenait garde à la peinture des colonnes.

Ce n'était pas notre première vie.

Quand je rentrai crotté du sang de nos frères, de nos ennemis,

Tu mis chauffer une bassine d'eau pure.

(Certains étaient nos frères et précisément nos ennemis, et certains,

Étrangers, cependant nos alliés.)

À la lueur du feu, je regardai tes mains étroites laver mes jambes écorchées.


Plus tard, tu allas seule,

Après ta dernière nuit de petite fille, jeter dans la flamme

Sur l'autel de la déesse impassible

Le lin naïf que tachait le premier sang qui nous séparait pour une vie.

Tu me suivis

Du regard déjà d'une femme quand je partis sous les oliviers,

Quand je repartis à la guerre.


5

Où en vérité, où donc partir ensemble ? Les poètes radotent.

Les poètes hâbleurs oublient toujours les bêtes bêlant à l'étable,

Le blé qui lève, les enfants affamés,

Go back to your husband!
I am not what you think. We are deceiving each other, lovely lady!
This is a treacherous season, when everything labors hidden in the earth.
But say something! speak! to refute at last the implacable
Certainty of your silence.


4

The temples were new. We watched out for the columns' fresh paint.
This wasn't our first life.
When I came back caked with the blood of our brothers, of our enemies,
You began to heat up a basin of pure water.
(Some of them were our brothers and in fact our enemies, and some,
Foreigners, nonetheless our allies.)
In the firelight, I watched your narrow hands wash my slashed legs.


Later, you went alone,
After your last night as a girlchild, to throw into the flames
On the altar of the impassive goddess
The innocent linen stained by the first blood that separated us for life.
You followed me
With what was already a woman's gaze when I left under the olive trees,
When I went back to war.


5

Where, in truth, might we depart together? The poets ramble on.
The braggart poets always forget the animals bleating in the barn,
The wheat rising, the hungry children,

Les arbres à greffer, les tuiles à poser après la bourrasque.
Nous avons toujours été ceux qui nourrissaient le feu et célébraient les fêtes
Du plus loin que je te connais, il a toujours fallu attendre, pour partir
Chacun de son côté, le dernier soir.

6

Il fut un temps où l'on savait que nous étions époux depuis toujours.
Je revois la demeure basse, la plate-forme nuptiale, avant de te laisser
Seule avec l'étranger captif.
Pour tromper les dieux, pour les lier au succès des semailles,
Pour leur faire croire qu'ils protégeaient enfin notre mariage prédestiné,
Le sorcier, entre le pauvre intrus et toi, me faisait coucher immobile
Comme un époux sacrifié.

7

Aller ailleurs ne mène pas au-delà de nos cœurs abusés,
Aller plus loin ne fait pas sortir de notre exil, aller ailleurs
Ne rouvre pas les portes ancestrales.
Viens, éteins la lampe, ferme tes yeux qui me connaissent par cœur,
Jardin fermé, profonde fontaine, immémorial amour, écoute
À travers ces corps sombres et doux se rechercher notre unité première.
Ailleurs est entre nos bras.

8

Tu connais, je connais cette patrie qui te ressemble,
Cette promesse de la nuit.

The trees to be grafted, the rooftiles laid after the squall.
We have always been the ones who fed the fire and kept the feast days.
As long as I've known you, we have always had to wait, then depart
In different directions, on the last night.


6

There was a time when it was known that we had always been a couple.
I can see the low dwelling, the nuptial platform, before I left you
Alone with the captive stranger.
To fool the gods, to link them to our successful sowing,
To make them believe that they were protecting our predestined marriage at last,
The magician had me lie between the poor intruder and you, motionless
Like a sacrificed spouse.


7

Going elsewhere doesn't take us beyond our misused hearts,
Going farther doesn't lead us out of our exile, going elsewhere
Doesn't reopen the ancestral portals.
Come, switch off the lamp, close your eyes that know me by heart,
Closed garden, deep fountain, love immemorial, hear
Through these dark and gentle bodies our first union seeking itself.
Elsewhere is in our arms.


8

You know, I know that country that resembles you,
That promise night makes.

Cette terre par-delà les eaux, cette demeure sur l'autre rive,
Ce pays toujours retrouvé.
Tu sais bien quel couloir nocturne nous ramène à la porte
Qui s'ouvrira sur notre ancien soleil.

Tu sais que l'ange te défend de l'ouvrir avant l'heure.
Ce serait trop facile.
Ce serait, dit-il, inutile d'écourter ce voyage, de revenir
Les mains vides
Comme un enfant qu'on envoyait aux champs porter nourriture
Et qui prit peur
Et revint, sans courage, sans amour nouveau, rapporter à la maison
Des larmes qui ne désaltèrent pas.


9

Reste encore dix minutes. On va t'appeler un taxi. Sois tranquille. Je suis
Partie de toi ; je suis toi-même ; tu ne t'appartiens pas. Il faut te retourner
Vers ce qu'ils appellent «chez toi».
Je sais. Tu reviendras, en cachette, mâcher avec moi, sans espoir,
L'amer et taciturne opium de notre identité perdue. Ne regrette rien.
Leurs tabous sont sans force. Mais non pas nos anges sévères. Il est écrit
Que nous aimerons autrui plus que nous-mêmes.

2/3/53

That land beyond the waters, that dwelling on the other bank,
That always rediscovered country.
You know very well what nocturnal passageway will lead us to the door
That will open on our ancient sun.
You know that the angel forbids you to open it before the predestined hour.

It would be too easy.
It would be, he says, useless to cut the voyage short, to return
Empty-handed
Like a child sent to carry food to the fields
And who took fright
And returned, without courage, without new love, to bring back to the house
Tears that quench no thirst.


9

Stay another ten minutes. I'll call you a taxi. Be calm. I'm
Part of you; I am you yourself; you aren't your own. You must go back
To what they call "home."
I know. You'll come back, to chew hopelessly with me
The bitter, silent opium of our lost likeness. Regret nothing.
Their taboos are powerless. But not our stern angels. It is written
That we shall love others more than ourselves.

# Femmes de la plaine : variations sur un thème

# Women of the Plain: Variations on a Theme

FEMMES DE LA PLAINE


les religieuses à grosses joues
rouges, à gros mollets, à gros
derrière le dimanche descendent chez
l'oncle vigneron manger la tarte aux prunes.
Il fait bleu depuis le sommet des monts
jusqu'au bas des coteaux. Mais tout cela c'est
la montagne dont parfois nous autres
gens de la plaine nous voyons au loin
une fenêtre heureuse briller dans un instant de soleil.
La plaine c'est autre chose. Entre les joncs,
parmi les roseaux glissent à long fil d'argent
et noires glissent les eaux dormantes
les eaux profondes où parfois une servante
se noie pour n'avoir pas épousé le
fils du meunier du maire ou du maréchal,
glissent les eaux dormantes sous
la chaleur de juillet équatorial
et la cigogne sur ses ailes étales
c'est en vain qu'elle survole
une demi-lieue de champs, tout est sec.
Les grenouilles d'herbe se sont blotties
sous les feuilles. Mais les eaux
glissent profondes pourtant habitées
de carpes, de brochets, de

## WOMEN OF THE PLAIN

           nuns with fat red
cheeks, fat calves, fat
bottoms go on Sundays to visit
the winemaker uncle and eat plum pies.
It's blue from the mountain peaks
down to the base of the hills. But all that's on
the mountain where we
plains folk sometimes see from a distance
a joyous window glitter in a moment's sunshine.
The plain is something else. Among the rushes,
among the reeds glide in a long black and
silver thread glide the dormant waters
the deep waters where sometimes a servant
girl drowns herself because she didn't marry the
miller's or the mayor's or the marshal's son,
glide the dormant waters beneath
the heat of equatorial July,
and the stork on spread wings
soars over a half-league of fields
in vain, everything is dry.
The tree frogs are curled up
under the leaves. But the waters
glide deep and inhabited
by carp, by pike, by

fantômes, de songes.
Toi qui debout sur la berge regardes
et sans armes vois passer sans
bruit, vois planer la buse, et le
Iapereau, toi qui regardes l'eau noire
qu'espères-tu donc ?

Odile, priez pour nous, femmes de la plaine
et plus particulièrement pour nous qui fûmes
filles de quelque lignage, apportant en dot
vignes, chasses, bons alignements
de houblon, de betteraves, de tabac,
bons comptoirs — bons tiroirs-caisses
de bonnes boucheries pâtisseries bijouteries
et maintes sommes pharmaciennes
perceptrices femmes du juge cantonal
et du docteur qui chaque jour en
2 tournées fait ses 100 kms pharmaciennes
notairesses femme de filateur et de
minotier et d'exportateur de vins.
Odile songez à nos longues journées
sur l'horizon de la plaine haut
et visible au loin pour l'enfant à vélo
revenant du collège, le sapin
qui par les soirs d'hiver gémit à
voix humaine. Une fois par mois
la couturière vient en journée dans la
grande chambre fourre-tout et l'enfant un soir

ghosts, by dreams.
You who watch standing on the shore
and unweaponed see them pass
silently, see the buzzard circle,
and the baby rabbit, you who watch the black water,
for what do you hope?

       Odile, pray for us, women of the plain,
and especially for those who were once
daughters of a certain lineage, bringing as dowry
vineyards, hunting grounds, good rows
of hops, of beets, of tobacco,
good businesses—good cash registers
of good butcher shops, bakeries, jeweler's shops,
and now we are pharmacists' wives,
tax collectors' wives, wives of the district judge
and of the doctor who does his daily 100 kilometers
in two rounds of visits, pharmacists' wives
notaries' wives, wives of the mill owner
and the miller and the wine exporter.
Odile think of our long days
on the plain's horizon high
and visible from a long way off to the child
on a bicycle coming back from middle school, the pine tree
that moans on winter nights with a
human voice. Once a month
the seamstress comes for a day's work in the
big storeroom and one evening the child

avait un début de fièvre et la nuit
se réveilla en gémissant. Hélas, nous le
sauvâmes, hélas nous le sauvâmes pour
les camps sibériens les crochets à porcs
des charcutiers bavarois les balles
de la jungle viet ou la montagne kabyle.

   le dimanche nous sortions
nous promener au-delà de la gare
en robes claires et souliers blanchis à
la craie, on rencontrait
la pharmacienne.
Pendant la fête des
rameaux la fête des
tentes les gosses, envoyés chez le
boulanger juif rapportaient par piles
de grandes plaques de pain azyme.
Hélas jour sans levain. Où est
passée notre jeunesse et l'album où
l'on recopiait des poésies de
Lamartine (Alphonse de) au
si beau nom si français si
distingué
jours sans levain. Et tout au profond
des eaux dormantes grandit à toute
petite vie la tumeur qui dans 20 ans
tuera.

had the start of a fever and that night
woke up moaning. Alas, we
saved him, alas we saved him for the
Siberian camps the meat hooks
of Bavarian butchers the bullets
in the Vietnamese jungle or the Kabyle mountains.

        on Sunday we'd go out
for a stroll beyond the railway station
in light-colored dresses, shoes whitened
with chalk, we'd meet
the pharmacist's wife.
On Palm Sunday, the day
of the tents, the kids, sent to the
Jewish baker, brought back stacks
of unleavened bread.
Alas day without yeast. Where has
our youth gone and the album where
we copied poems by
Lamartine (Alphonse de) his so
beautiful name so French so
elegant
days without yeast. And in the deepest
dormant waters grows so slowly
but surely the tumor which in twenty years
will kill.

## MORT DE LA FEMME DU PHARMACIEN

Par temps clair
après la pluie, de la
lucarne du grenier, on voyait
les villages de la montagne, les villages dans les
vignes, les villages heureux. Et dans notre plaine, par-delà
les houblons, les blés, les champs de tabac ou maïs
les peupliers en file sur la route du Sud.

Odile, priez pour nous !
L'hiver est long. Pour que les enfants
allant à l'école puissent quitter leurs sabots,
puissent, leurs sabots à la main, courir en chaussons sur
cent mètres de terre séchée au soleil, il faut
attendre le retour des cigognes.

Odile, protégez-nous.
L'année est longue. En été, parfois,
encore jeunes, nous allions par les soirs clairs
marcher sur la route jusqu'au point où derrière les houblons
disparaît même le clocher. Sous les pommiers,
les lapins aux longues oreilles étaient
assis par couples.

Odile, donnez-nous courage !
Il a fallu attendre d'être vieux pour

## DEATH OF THE PHARMACIST'S WIFE

In clear weather
after the rain, from the
attic skylight, we could see
the mountain villages, the villages in the
vineyards, the fortunate villages. And on our plain, beyond
the hops, the wheat, the tobacco fields or cornfields,
the poplars lined up on the road toward the south.

Odile, pray for us!
The winter is long. For the children
going to school to take off their wooden clogs,
and, with clogs in hands, run in slippers on
a hundred meters of sun-dried earth, we must
wait for the storks to return.

Odile, protect us.
The year is long. Sometimes, in summer,
when we were still young, we would go on clear evenings
to walk out on the road to the spot where behind the hop fields
even the steeple disappeared. Under the apple trees
long-eared rabbits were
sitting in couples.

Odile, give us courage!
It wasn't until we grew old that

une fois l'an aller faire une cure à Aix et
chaque matin, assis devant le kiosque, écouter le violoniste.
Il jouait comme dans les films. Odile, donnez-nous
courage, donnez-nous espérance.

Eaux calmes et profondes
lentement à la dérive à travers les
prés humides et gras, vers le jeune Rhin, eaux
où dérive sans bruit la barque plate et noire du pêcheur.
J'ai écouté le silence des eaux au soir, tandis
que s'élevait bientôt le coassement des grenouilles.

Barque plate et noire comme les
heures de l'attente. Les enfants grandissent et
cesse le temps où l'enfant premier-né croit que sa
mère est une déesse qui sait tout. Les enfants grandissent,
partent au lycée, à la guerre, partent dans les
villes, partent à la guerre que ne comprennent pas les femmes.
Et reviennent, bruyants, distraits. Les enfants
grandissent, qui étaient doux et blonds et sans défense
contre mon corsage, sinon la défense déjà
de ce je ne sais quel secret qu'apporte avec elle en naissant
semble-t-il qu'apporte chaque âme.

Odile, priez pour nous !

Faite de tant de longues années vides,
Odile, que la vie est courte et de peu de soleil !

we could go once a year to Aix to take the cure and,
sitting by the kiosk every morning, listen to the violinist.
He played as they do in films. Odile, give us
courage, give us hope.

Deep calm rivers
slowly drifting across the
damp muddy plains, toward the young Rhine, waters
where the fisherman's flat black boat drifts silently.
In the evening I listened to the silence of the waters, where
soon the frogs' croaking would begin.

Boat flat and black as the
hours of waiting. The children grow up and
gone is the time when the firstborn thought his
mother was an all-knowing goddess. The children grow
and leave for high school, for war, leave for the
city, go off to wars that women don't understand.
And return, noisy, distracted. The children
grow up, who were gentle and blond and defenseless
held to my bodice, or with the sole defense
of I don't know what secret that each one brings at birth
that it seems each soul brings.

Odile, pray for us!

Made of so many long empty years,
Odile, how short life is and how little sun!

Odile, que les nuits sont longues !
Odile, que la guerre est longue et la vieillesse
parmi les lettres rares des enfants trop vite grandis.

Odile, fille de puissant seigneur, naquit aveugle.
Elle fut peu aimée.
Mais qu'est la clôture du cloître
pour celle qui est clôturée tout à l'intérieur d'elle-même,
qu'est le silence et le froid sinon protection, espace,
nuit où le cœur essaie ses ailes ? Odile, dans le flanc de la
pierre rose et friable, ayant fait jaillir une source fraîche
y lava ses yeux et vit.

Odile, qui fûtes aveugle et peu aimée,
priez pour nous aussi, femmes, encore jeunes,
dans les villages de la plaine. La journée est longue,
l'hiver est long, l'année est longue et tant d'années
longues et vides font une vie si courte !

Odile, guidez-nous.
Dans ces soudains repères,
Odile, donnez-nous la main et dessillez nos yeux.
Odile, priez pour les villages de la plaine.

Odile, how long the nights are!
Odile, how long war lasts, and old age
　　　among rare letters from too quickly grown children.

　　　Odile, daughter of a powerful lord, was born blind.
　　　She was not beloved.
　　　But what is the enclosure of a cloister
to one who is enclosed within herself,
what are silence and cold but protection, space,
night where the heart tries its wings? Odile, from the flank of the
rosy friable stone, made a cool spring gush forth
washed her eyes in it and could see.

　　　Odile, you who were blind and not beloved,
　　　　pray for us also, women, still young,
in the villages of the plain. The days are long,
the winter is long, the year is long, and so many long
and empty years make such a short life!

　　　　　Odile, guide us!
　　　　Among these sudden landmarks,
　　　Odile, take our hands and open our eyes.
Odile, pray for the villages of the plain.

## MORT DE LA FEMME DU PERCEPTEUR

Le docteur a prescrit un tonique pour le cœur
pour faire durer l'agonisante jusqu'à l'arrivée d'une fille distraite
d'un fils longtemps aimé de loin.

Le vent d'Italie qui descend des glaciers
à peine tiédi vient tourmenter les branches du grand sapin
qui gémissait déjà les soirs où venait la couturière.

Il fut un temps où elle riait aux fenêtres
d'une pension aux rives du Léman vouée à former des
filles de famille copiant dans un cahier des poésies
de Coppée et Sully Prudhomme le vase brisé.

Jonas sa mère étant pauvrette et ancienne
ses os déjà rongés allant aux eaux soigner en vain
la sciatique qui cache un cancer
Jonas descend le plateau vers le Rhin nocturne
et troue de phares les bourgades préservées.

C'est ici le lieu qu'il faut choisir. Il est tard.

*Schambadiss, gridawiss*
*himmelbläu, katzegräu.*

Le vent par-dessus les glaciers accouru du désert
vient à peine fraîchi tourmenter les branches du grand sapin

## DEATH OF THE TAX COLLECTOR'S WIFE

The doctor has prescribed a tonic for the heart
to make the dying woman last till a distracted daughter's arrival,
a son loved so long from afar.

The Italian wind that descends barely warmed
from the glaciers comes to torment the branches of the tall pine
that was already moaning the nights the seamstress came.

There was a time when she laughed beside the windows
of a boarding school on the banks of Lac Léman meant to form
bourgeois daughters copying poems in a notebook
by Coppée and Sully Prudhomme the shattered vase.

Jonah, his mother being poor and old,
her bones already gnawed, taking the waters to treat in vain
the sciatica that hid a cancer,
Jonah comes down the plateau toward the nocturnal Rhine
and pierces the preserved towns with headlights.

Here is the place that must be chosen. It is late.

*Schambadiss, gridawiss*
*himmelbläu, katzegräu.*

The wind that rushed here from the desert above the glaciers
comes barely cooled to torment the tall pine's branches.

Comment dormir quand tout est en travail et en
peine de se perpétuer ?

Sur les eaux lentes et lisses, les barques noires, les barques plates
demain à lente gaffe poussées vers les foins sur la berge
sont pareilles à l'âme indéfiniment amarrées.

L'année est lente avant de ramener
la fille distraite, le fils longtemps aimé de loin
les enfants qui riaient parmi ses bras
écrivent rarement à la femme du percepteur.

Odile, aidez-nous à ne pas accepter
les longues nuits auprès de l'époux qui ronfle
et sous son bonnet de coton accumule
les intérêts des intérêts de ses longues prudences.

Odile, qui parfois semblez nous faire signe
quand après l'orage les villages sur la montagne
brillent au-dessus des vignes
à brefs éclairs de lointaines fenêtres heureuses,
Odile qui après la longue nuit avez trouvé
la source qui fait voir, Odile, ne me laissez pas oublier
la jeunesse l'album où l'on copiait des poésies,
la broderie d'une lente aiguille encore pleine d'attente
et mon sang frais se mêlait au fil rouge
sur le drap écru parmi les coiffes et les
cigognes au bec incongru.

How can you sleep when everything is in labor, toiling
to perpetuate itself?

On the slow, smooth waters, the black boats, the flat boats
that pushed tomorrow with slow hooks toward the hay on the riverbank
are like the soul, indefinitely anchored.

The year goes slowly before it brings back
the distracted daughter, the son so long loved from afar
the children who used to laugh in her arms
rarely write to the tax collector's wife.

Odile, help us not to accept
those long nights beside a spouse who snores
while beneath his cotton nightcap the interest
on the interest of his long prudence accumulates.

Odile, who sometimes seemed to give us a sign,
when, after a storm, mountain villages
glistened beyond the vineyards
in brief flashes from fortunate windows,
Odile, you who found, after the long night,
the source that granted sight, Odile, let me not forget
youth, the album where we copied poems,
embroidering with a slow needle still full of waiting
and my fresh blood mingled with red thread
on the unbleached linen among the headdresses and the
storks with incongruous beaks.

Viendra-t-il avec le vent plus rapide, de Milan, de Venise
de Tunis, l'enfant longtemps souhaité.
Parfois il a oublié le télégramme pour ma fête
le baisers lettre suit qui ne venait jamais.
Quel héritage ai-je bien pu transmettre sans le perdre.

La beauté est de peu de prix, sinon
pour attirer plus vite le geôlier. Ô captive
parmi les saisons le tonneau de choux
frais coupés sur la râpe aux premiers givres d'octobre
quand l'hirondelle soudain partie on se réveille
dans le premier silence de l'arrière-saison.

Les barques plates et noires sont amarrées
gondoles qui ne serviront jamais à des fêtes.

Odile aidez le cœur quand il feuillette
dans l'album de photo les jaunes reflets
de printemps passés les sourires pour le principe.

Odile la plaine est sans merci. La nuit
se plaignent les grenouilles en peine de perpétuité.
La cigogne va glisser dans d'autres cheminées son long bec inconvenant
Le pommier a versé sur l'herbe ses dernières pommes
avant l'orage qui le brisera.

Parfois on partait en excursions dans les montagnes
montant depuis la gare de la vallée le sentier
qui souffle une haleine fraîche parmi les arbres.

Will he come with the swiftest wind from Milan, from Venice,
from Tunis, the child so wished for.
Sometimes he would forget the telegram for my birthday
the kisses letter will follow that never came.
What heritage could I have left him without losing him.

Beauty isn't good for much, if not
to attract the jailer more quickly. O captive
among the seasons, the barrel of fresh
cabbages grated at October's first frost,
when, with the swallows suddenly gone, we awake
in the first silence of the changed season.

The flat black boats are anchored,
gondolas that will float for no festivities.

Odile, help the heart when it leafs through
the photo album, the yellow reflections
of past springs, the smiles smiled on principle.

Odile, the plain is merciless. At night
frogs struggling to reproduce complain.
The stork will slip his long improper beak into other chimneys.
The apple tree has spilled its last apples on the grass
before the storm that will break it.

Sometimes we would leave for an excursion in the mountains,
climbing up from the railway station in the valley on a path
that exhales a cool breath among the trees.

Odile, les barques ne sont jamais parties
et l'on s'est fatigué d'attendre
l'héritage venu trop tard pour changer les vies gâchées.

L'horloge marche à gros sabots, la pendule
ancienne à gros sabots mesure la nuit qui
lentement dérive à peine comme une barque
obstinément amarrée contre la traction de l'eau noire.

Qu'il est dur de rompre l'amarre ! Qu'il est long
le temps pour la traction de l'eau d'arracher
la chaîne rouillée au bord des herbages brûlés.

Le tulle et la cretonne et le tussor
furent sous l'aiguille de la couturière en journée
des voiles dérisoires pour un départ toujours futur
tandis que gémissait le grand sapin dans le
soir de novembre où l'enfant fiévreux se plaint en rêve
de toutes les séparations vers lesquelles il grandit.

Odile, aidez-nous quand la jeunesse
à ne pas se perdre s'est gaspillée quand la nuit
comme jadis en travail craque vers un
matin vide parmi le silence soudain qui
suit le départ des hirondelles.

Doux nid si rond couleur de terre fait de
terre et de salive pendu sous l'aisselle du vieux toit
nid vide pour les sarcasmes des moineaux.

Odile, the boats never departed,
and we grew tired waiting for
an inheritance come too late to change wasted lives.

The clock walks on in its wooden clogs, the old
grandfather clock in its heavy clogs measures the night that
barely, slowly drifts like a boat
stubbornly anchored against the black water's tugging.

How hard it is to break loose from the moorings! How long
it takes for the water's tugging to loosen
the rusty chain beside the burnt pastures.

Tulle and cretonne and raw silk
became, under the needle of the seamstress who did day work,
pathetic sails for an always future departure,
while the tall pine moaned in the
November evening where the feverish child complained
dreaming of all the separations he was growing toward.

Odile, help us when youth
for fear of losing itself, was wasted when the night
cracks as once in labor toward an
empty morning in the sudden silence
that follows the swallows' departure.

Sweet nest so round earth-colored made of
mud and saliva hung in the old roof's armpit
nest empty to the sparrows' sarcasms.

Ils n'ont pas su nous dire comment partir
mais seulement comment faire ces
longs ouvrages de notre captivité.

Il fallait bien pourtant garder le feu le toit
le grain la cave le grenier le buffet
Henri II le bahut breton le linoléum
garder la. huche et l'armoire aux confitures
garder le lit pour lequel on broda
12 fois 12 initiales à fil de soie vermeille.

Il fallait bien pourtant attendre
la justification qui maintenant ne viendra plus
que maintenant on ne verra plus. Ô enfant oublieux !

Le cœur à gros sabots arpente les prairies nocturnes
les mains ne peuvent plus retenir que cette seule main
longtemps désirée si longtemps lointaine le cœur
à gros sabots piétine sur la berge de l'eau lisse et
noire et lente qu'il faudra traverser bientôt.

Qui jamais est revenu de ces villages inimaginables ?
Tous ceux qui devant nous ont traversé
quand ont-ils réussi à se faire entendre
parmi le long gémissement des arbres tourmentés de vent

Pourtant, toute rivière a deux bords toute rivière
coule entre deux prairies. Je sais je crois

They could not tell us how to leave
but only how to execute these
long works of our captivity.

And yet the fire had to be tended the roof
the grain the cellar the attic the Henri II
sideboard the Breton chest the linoleum
tend to the bread box the jam cupboard
tend to the bed for which we embroidered
12 initials 12 times in vermilion silk thread.

And yet it was necessary to wait
for a justification that now will no longer arrive
that now we will not see again. Oh neglectful child!

The heart in its heavy clogs paces nocturnal plains
the hands can hold nothing but that singular hand
so long desired and far away so long the heart
in its heavy clogs straggles on the bank of the smooth and
black and slow water it soon must cross.

Who ever returned from those unimaginable villages?
All those who crossed before us, when
have they managed to make themselves heard
among the long moans of wind-tormented trees?

Yet every river has two banks every river
runs between two plains. I know I believe

que mon Sauveur est vivant. Au bord du caveau vide
les soldats dorment comme des corps putréfiés déjà.
Ce long effort cette longue patience
quel jour ont-ils suivi que je ne verrai plus ?
quel fruit tardif quelle moisson longtemps ajournée
quelle vendange de raisins longtemps demeurés acides ?

Quel jardinier bizarre est le maître qui
fait attendre à celui qui plante un arbre qu'il soit mort
avant de laisser mûrir le fruit.

10/9/56

that my Redeemer liveth. Beside the empty tomb
the soldiers sleep like already putrefied corpses.
This long straining this long patience,
what day did they follow that I will no longer see
what late fruit what long-postponed harvest
what picking of grapes that stayed acid for so long?

What a strange gardener the master who
makes the one who plants a tree wait until he is dead
for the fruit to ripen.

Le vent par-dessus les glaciers accouru du désert
vient à peine fraîchi tourmenter les branches du grand sapin.
Quand tout est en travail comment dormir, comment aussi
mourir?

Sur les eaux lentes et lisses, les barques noires, les barques plates
demain à lente gaffe poussées vers les foins sur la berge
sont, pareilles à l'âme, indéfiniment amarrées.

L'année est longue avant de ramener
la fille distraite, le fils longtemps aimé de loin.
Les enfants qui riaient parmi ses bras et sur ses seins
écrivent rarement à la femme du percepteur.

Odile, qui parfois semblez nous faire signe
quand après l'orage les villages de la montagne
brillent au-dessus des vignes
à brefs éclairs de lointaines fenêtres heureuses,
Odile, aidez-nous à ne pas regretter, à ne pas oublier notre jeunesse.

La beauté est de peu de prix, sinon
comme un dernier appel qui ne sera pas entendu. Ô captive
parmi les saisons, le tonneau de choux
frais coupés dans la cave aux premiers givres d'octobre,

## WOMEN OF THE PLAIN: IV

The wind above the glaciers that rushed from the desert
comes, barely cooled, to worry the tall pine tree's branches.
When everything is in labor, how can you sleep, how
can you die?

On the slow smooth waters, the black boats, the flat boats,
tomorrow nudged with slow hooks toward bales of hay on the shore
are, like the soul, indefinitely anchored.

The year drags on, before it will bring back
the distracted daughter, the son loved so long from afar.
The children who laughed in her arms, on her breasts
rarely write to the tax collector's wife.

Odile, you who sometimes seem to give us a sign,
when, after a storm, mountain villages
glistened beyond the vineyards
in brief flashes from fortunate windows,
Odile, help us not to forget, regret our youth.

Beauty isn't worth much, except
as a last plea that will not be heard. O captive
among the seasons, the barrel of fresh-cut
cabbages in the cellar at October's first frost,

quand l'hirondelle soudain partie, on se réveille
dans le premier silence de l'arrière-saison.

Odile, la plaine est sans merci. La nuit
se plaignent les grenouilles en peine de se perpétuer.
La cigogne dans d'autres cheminées va plonger son long bec lubrique.

La pendule ancienne à gros sabots, le cœur à pas lourds
mesure la nuit qui lentement dérive à peine, comme une barque
obstinément amarrée contre la traction de l'eau noire.

Qu'il est dur de rompre l'amarre ! Qu'il est long
le temps pour la traction de l'eau d'arracher
la chaîne depuis longtemps rouillée qui retient à la berge !

Le tulle et la cretonne et le tussor
le crêpe georgette et les cotonnades imprimées avec discrétion
firent sous l'aiguille de la couturière venue en journée
des voiles dérisoires pour un départ toujours futur,
tandis que gémissait le grand sapin dans le
soir de novembre où l'enfant fiévreux se plaint en vain
de toutes les séparations vers lesquelles il grandit.

Odile, aidez-nous quand la jeunesse
à ne pas se perdre s'est gaspillée, quand la nuit
comme jadis en travail craque et geint vers un matin vide
parmi le silence qui suit le départ des hirondelles.
Doux nid, si rond, couleur de terre, fait de

when, with the swallows suddenly gone, we awake
in the first silence of the changed season.

Odile, the plain is merciless. At night
frogs at a loss to reproduce complain.
The stork will plunge its long lewd beak in other chimneys.

The grandfather clock in wooden clogs, the heavy-footed heart
measure the night which slowly, barely, drifts like a boat
stubbornly anchored against the black water's tugging.

How hard it is to break loose from the moorings. How long
it takes for the water's tugging to drag away
the rusted chain that tethers to the shore!

Tulle and cretonne and raw silk
georgette and discreetly printed cottons
became, under the needles of the seamstress come for a day's work,
ludicrous sails for an always delayed departure
while the tall pine moaned in the
November night where the feverish child vainly protested
all the separations he was growing toward.

Odile, help us when youth
for fear of losing itself is wasted, when night
cracks and moans as it did in labor toward an empty morning
in the silence following the swallows' departure.
Soft nest, so round, earth colored, made of

terre et de salive, de boue et de satin, pendu sous l'aisselle du toit,
nid vide désormais pour les sarcasmes des moineaux.

Le cœur à gros sabots arpente les prairies nocturnes
piétine sur la berge de l'eau lisse et noire et lente
qu'il faut traverser bientôt.

Pourtant, toute rivière a deux bords, toute rivière
coule entre deux prairies. Au bord du caveau vide
les soldats dorment comme des corps putréfiés
tandis que se déroule dans une lumière jaune
la chrysalide surnaturelle, la chrysalide parvenue
à l'éclosion de sa nature dernière et première.

Ô terre partout riche et pourtant légère, labourée à deux bœufs,
ô fruits épars sur l'automne des routes, ô filles raisonnables
dont le ventre se rendort si vite après les délires du solstice !
Odile, ô fille aveugle qui lava ses yeux à la source
et vit la blondeur nouvelle et le bleu marial
dans l'altitude où passe à grands battements d'aile peu pressée,
la lubrique et perpétuelle cigogne.

Cigogne, tel un phénix, sur son nid d'épines,
très fond, en forme de couronne amère.

earth and saliva, mud and satin, hung in the roof's armpit,
nest from now on empty to the sparrows' sarcasms.

The heart in its heavy clogs paces the nighttime plains,
lingers on the shore of the smooth black slow waters
which it soon must cross.

Yet every river has two banks, every river
runs between two prairies. Outside the empty tomb
soldiers sleep like putrefying corpses
while in a yellow light the uncanny
chrysalis unwinds, the chrysalis come
to term of its last and first nature.

O earth, rich everywhere and yet light, plowed by two oxen,
O sparse fruits of an autumn of roads, O sensible girls
whose wombs doze off so quickly after the frenzy of solstice!
Odile, O blind girl who washed your eyes at the source
and saw new blondness and Marial blue
at the height where, with great unhurried wingbeats
the lascivious perpetual stork passes by.

Stork, like a phoenix on its nest of thorns,
round, shaped like a bitter crown.

# DERNIÈRE NUIT DE LA PHARMACIENNE

Le vent par-dessus les glaciers accouru du désert
vient à peine fraîchi tourmenter les branches du grand sapin.
Quand tout est en travail, comment dormir, comment aussi
mourir ?

Sur les eaux lentes et lisses, les barques plates,
les barques noires sont, pareilles
à l'âme, presque indéfiniment amarrées.

L'année est longue avant de ramener
la fille distraite, le fils longtemps aimé de loin.
Les enfants qui riaient dans ses bras et sur ses seins
écrivent rarement à la femme du pharmacien,
même pour des remèdes.

La beauté est de peu de prix, sinon
comme un dernier appel qui ne sera plus entendu. Ô captive
parmi les saisons, le tonneau de choux frais
coupés dans la cave aux premiers givres d'octobre,
quand l'hirondelle soudain partie, on se réveille
dans le premier silence de l'arrière-saison.

Odile, la plaine est sans merci. La nuit
se plaignent les grenouilles en peine de se perpétuer.
La cigogne dans d'autres cheminées plonge son long bec lubrique.

# THE LAST NIGHT OF THE PHARMACIST'S WIFE

The wind that rushed here from the desert above the glaciers
comes barely cooled to torment the tall pine tree's branches.
When everything is in labor, how can you sleep, how
can you die?

On the slow smooth waters, the flat boats,
the black boats are, like the soul,
almost permanently moored.

The year grows long before it brings back
the distracted daughter, the son long loved from afar.
The children who laughed in her arms, on her breasts
rarely write to the pharmacist's wife,
even to ask for remedies.

Beauty is cheap, except
as a last appeal that will no longer be heard. O captive
between the seasons, the barrel of fresh cabbages
cut in the cellar in October's first frosts,
when with the swallows suddenly gone, you
wake in the first silence of late fall.

Odile, the plain is merciless. At night
frogs at a loss to reproduce complain.
The stork plunges its long lecherous beak down other chimneys.

Les pendules à gros sabots, le cœur à pas lourds
mesurent la nuit qui dérive à peine. Qu'il est dur
de rompre l'amarre ! Qu'il est long
le temps pour la traction de l'eau d'arracher
la chaîne qui depuis tant de temps retient à la berge !

Le cœur à gros sabots arpente les prairies nocturnes,
piétine sur la berge de l'eau
que très bientôt il faudra traverser.

The clock with heavy wooden clogs, the heart with heavy steps
measure the night which barely drifts. How hard it is
to break loose from the moorings! How long it takes
for the water's traction to tear loose
the chain that for so long grasped the riverbank!

The heart in its heavy clogs paces the nocturnal plains,
stands shifting its feet on the shore of the water
which very soon it must cross.

# Jonas

# Jonah

Ils ont habité avec nous dans la gueule de la baleine.
La baleine les a crachés sur l'autre rivage :

Les timides.

Les gauchers.

Celui qui était albinos et bègue.

Les myopes. Les méfiants, les malins.

Et ce grand garçon qui avait toujours soif,

toujours sommeil.

Regardent-ils parfois par-dessus notre épaule ?

Depuis qu'ils sont partis, nous n'avons vu personne.

Sommes-nous aveugles ? Ou bien

« spiritisme, religion de nègres », écrit,

dans quelque périodique exquis, un Révérend Père.

Pourtant,

s'ils regardaient, parfois, par-dessus notre épaule ?

Ou bien, quittant le rivage de la mer intermédiaire,

se sont-ils avancés depuis longtemps

dans l'intérieur des terres spirituelles ?

Le sorcier noir sait appeler, sait, quand elles voudraient

s'en aller, retenir, ramener les ombres, les âmes.

Qui de nous saurait appeler

saurait ramener

## OPENING INVOCATION

They lived with us in the belly of the whale.
The whale spat them out on the other shore:

The shy ones.
The left-handed.
The one who was albino and stammered.
The nearsighted. The distrustful, the cunning.
And that tall boy who was always thirsty,

always sleepy.

Do they sometimes look over our shoulders?
      Since they've gone, we've seen no one.
         Are we blind? Or
      "spiritualism, that negro religion," writes,
      in some delightful periodical, a Reverend Father.

And yet
if they were looking, sometimes, over our shoulders?

Or otherwise, leaving the shore of the intermediate sea,
      has it been a while since they've gone ahead
         into the interior of lands of the spirit?
The black sorcerer knows how to call, knows, even when they want
      to depart, how to call back shadows, souls.
      Who among us would know how to call,
         know how to bring back

l'ombre de John,
de Bernard,
de Maurice ?


En l'honneur de Monseigneur Saint Maurice
colonel romain qui commanda la légion thébaine,
martyr, fête le 22 septembre,
l'abbé de Saint-Maurice-en-Valais, évêque de Bethléem
porte mémorial ruban de moire écarlate.


Mais Maurice
qui n'allait plus à la synagogue, ne peignait plus de fleurs,
ne peignait plus qu'un pan de mur, une porte ouverte, un peu
de lumière d'atelier par une porte entrebâillée,
des verticales, la ligne d'horizon du plancher,
Maurice qui se privait du vert, du bleu,
qui de nos morts servira de guide à Maurice ?
Qui de nous vivants saura faire un feu pour Maurice ?
Que brûlerons-nous de nous-mêmes
pour faire le feu spirituel ayant pouvoir
de réchauffer, de délivrer Maurice ?


(Une tradition, t'en souvient-il, assure que les suicidés
souffrent longtemps, emprisonnés dans des glaces mentales,
de tout voir, sans pouvoir jamais agir, avertir, aider.)


Ombre,
qui regardes par-dessus mon épaule
que puis-je faire pour toi ?

the shadow of John,
of Bernard,
of Maurice?

In honor of Monseigneur Saint Maurice
Roman colonel who commanded the Theban legion,
martyr, his feast on September 22,
the abbot of Saint-Maurice-en-Valais, bishop of Bethlehem,
wears a ribbon of scarlet moiré.

But Maurice,
who no longer went to the synagogue, no longer painted flowers,
painted only a patch of wall, an open door, a bit
of the studio's light through a half-open door,
verticals, the floor's horizon line,
Maurice, who deprived himself of green, of blue,
who among our dead will serve as guide for Maurice?
Who among our living will know to light a flame for Maurice?
What will we burn of ourselves
to feed the spiritual flame that will be able
to warm, to deliver Maurice?

(A tradition, do you remember, claims that suicides,
frozen in mental ice, suffer at length
from seeing everything, never able to act, avert, aid.)

Shadow,
looking over my shoulder,
what can I do for you?

Il n'y a point ici d'ombre, mais seulement
la peine et le travail des hommes vivants,
la longueur du temps, la résistance de la seule matière.
Mais qui dira
si les ombres parmi nous
ne sont pas à leur tour penchées
sur ce même travail inépuisable ?

Ombre, que puis-je pour toi?
Avec mes yeux bornés, mes yeux vivants,
avec mes mains obtuses, vivantes,
avec ce corps, avec ce temps qui m'est laissé,
Ombre, veux-tu que je regarde
pour toi
ces visages, ces paysages ?
veux-tu que je touche
pour toi
ces fleurs, ces cheveux, ces choses ?

veux-tu que j'essaie
avec toi
de soulever un peu du lourd fardeau accumulé ?

Qu'as-tu fait de ton frère Maurice ?

J'étais ailleurs. Je n'ai rien entendu.
Je n'écoutais pas. Je me regardais dans un miroir.
Ce n'est pas moi qui ai ouvert le gaz.
Je n'ai rien fait pour mon frère Maurice.

There is no shadow here, only
     the effort and the work of living men,
time's length, the resistance of mere matter.
                    But who will say
          if the shadows among us
      are not bent in their turn
   over the same inexhaustible task?


Shadow, what can I do for you?
     With my short-sighted eyes, my living eyes,
         with my stubborn, living hands,
     with this body, this time left to me.
Shadow, do you want me to look
     in your place
         at these faces, these fields?
   do you want me to touch
     in your place
         these flowers, this hair, these things?


   do you want me to try
     with you
     to lift this heavy burden even a little?

What have you done with your brother Maurice?


     I was somewhere else. I heard nothing.
     I wasn't listening. I was looking in the mirror.
     I wasn't the one who turned on the gas.
     I did nothing for my brother Maurice.

Ombre, qu'ai-je à t'offrir ?
        Quel pain ?
Je n'ai pas défriché, pas labouré, je n'ai pas semé,
Je n'ai tracé que des chemins de poussière et
    mon sillage parfois sur la mer qui oublie tout passage.
Quel pain, sinon de ténèbre et de séparation ?
        Quelle eau ?
Je n'ai pas marché vers les eaux désirables,
je n'ai pas de quoi te donner à boire.


            Et Bernard
            qui toujours dormait de tout son long
        à plat ventre, bras en avant comme le
        nageur de crawl dans l'eau profonde du sommeil,
qu'as-tu fait de ton frère Bernard ?


        Il ne m'a pas appelé.
    Quand je suis incapable de me garder moi-même
        Comment serais-je le gardien de mon frère ?
    De quoi porterai-je témoignage
        sinon de mon injuste sursis ?


Ombre, tu te souviens ? Il fut un temps
        où comme les femmes à l'heure de leur accouchement
    nous regardions d'un même regard et la mort et la vie.


        Il m'importe peu
        si l'univers a forme d'œuf ou de

Shadow, what can I offer you?
          What bread?
I did not prepare the ground, did not plow, did not sow,
I marked out only paths of dust and
sometimes my wake on the sea that forgets all passings.
What bread, but that of darkness and separation?
          What water?
I did not walk toward refreshing waters,
I have nothing to offer you to drink.


        And Bernard
           who always slept stretched out full length
        on his belly, one arm extended like a
      swimmer doing the crawl in sleep's deep waters,
what have you done with your brother Bernard?


      He did not call out to me.
    When I cannot keep myself
      how can I be my brother's keeper?
To what shall I bear witness
      if not my own unjust reprieve?

Shadow, do you remember? There was a time
      when, like women in labor,
we looked at life and death with the same gaze.


      What does it matter to me if
      the universe is shaped like an egg or

boomerang. Notre pays à nous, c'est
ce maigre rivage où nous voici jetés,
notre voyage à nous, c'est
le voyage dans la baleine.

Ombre, tu te souviens :
Ce dimanche de mai.
L'église d'un village d'argile et de décrépitude.
Six cents feux. Combien d'âmes ?
Nous étions debout
casque accroché au ceinturon,
masque qui servait à Bernard de garde-manger,
bidon rempli des sacrements de l'Intendance,
nous étions debout,
vêtus de cuir, de fer, de feutre,
vêtus de peau mortelle.
Nous écoutions ces voix d'enfants.


Comme le cerf brame après la fraîcheur des eaux...
Je n'ai pas eu soif pour mes frères. Et peu à peu
me gagnent la broussaille de l'âge, la ronce du mépris,
et cette solitude qui n'est que paresse, comparée à
ton dur hivernage dans la banquise mentale.
Ombre, voici que
je voudrais avoir eu soif, pour toi, depuis l'origine du temps.
Le cerf est
stupide, le cerf se bat pour
la biche la plus gluante, le cerf

like a boomerang? Our only country is
this sparse shore where we've been thrown up,
our only journey is
the journey in the belly of the whale.

Shadow, do you remember:
That Sunday in May.
The church in a village all clay and decay.
Six hundred hearths. How many souls?
We were standing
with our helmets hooked to our belts,
gas mask that Bernard used as his bread box,
canteens filled with the Supply Corps' sacraments,
we were standing,
dressed in leather, in iron, in felt,
dressed in our mortal skin.
We listened to those children's voices.

As the stag calls after the waters' coolness . . .
I did not thirst for my brothers. And little by little
the underbrush of age caught at me, the thorns, the scorn,
and that solitude which is only laziness, compared to
your hard wintering in mental ice floes.
Shadow, I would have
wanted to thirst, for you, since the beginning of time.
The stag is
stupid, the stag fights for
the doe in heat, the stag

empêtre sa ramure dans les sous-bois, mais le cerf
brame à la recherche des eaux vivantes. Voici que
je n'ai accumulé que la citerne de la mélancolie,
la fontaine de Narcisse, qui ne désaltère personne,
                    et ces larmes
                            pleurées sur moi-même.


Ombre, tu te souviens :
        (toi qui peut-être souffres de notre peu de soif)
                    ces voix d'enfants.
                        distribué le pain dont on assure qu'il fut béni
            ces voix d'enfants,
            ces mots de notre obscurité, ces mots
        de notre misérable et nécessaire devoir,
ces voix
        essayant d'offrir quelque nom qui pût convenir :


SEIGNEUR
        chef de guerre, chef de clan,
        fils de l'ancien totem,
        roi sacrifié pour nos semailles,
        père qui défend et qui punit,


HAGIOS O THEOS : SANCTUS DEUS
        créateur de la tarentule et du serpent,
        inventeur des muqueuses et des sphincters,
        chimiste de l'albumine et de l'ammoniaque,

catches his antlers in the underbrush, but the stag
bells in search of the living waters. While I have
only filled up the cistern of melancholy,
Narcissus's fountain, which quenches no one's thirst,
and these tears
wept over myself.

Shadow, do you remember:
(you who suffer, perhaps, from our lack of thirst)
those children's voices,
the bread distributed, said to be blessed,
those children's voices,
those words of our darkness, those words
of our wretched and necessary duty,
those voices
trying to suggest some suitable name:

LORD
lord of war, head of the clan,
son of the ancient totem,
king sacrificed for our sowing,
father who forbids and punishes,

HAGIOS O THEOS: SANCTUS DEUS
creator of the tarantula and the snake,
inventor of sphincters and mucus membranes,
chemist of albumen and ammonia,

HAGIOS, ISCHYROS : SANCTUS, FORTIS
illusionniste, escamoteur,
enfant qui fait des bulles d'hydrogène,
ovaire d'une seule menstrue pondant les galaxies,

DEUS SABAOTH : SEIGNEUR DES ARMÉES
Seigneur des cohortes spirituelles,
Seigneur aussi de notre déroute,
Seigneur aussi de nos nuits vers la mort, vers la vie.
« Emportez-moi » criaient des voix dans la nuit,
Seigneur de notre première halte
dans la joie d'être vivants,
dans la honte d'être vivants
aux quatre coins de ce drap noir tendu,
le drap du Requiem pour tant de corps absents,
ce drap vide que nous tenions : un soldat,
un sergent, un capitaine, un officier général
tenant aux quatre coins
ce drap creusé sous le poids invisible
de tant de cendres laissées derrière nous.

La nuit dans les chars qui rouillent sur
les hauts de Meuse, l'araignée tisse, la fourmi
à longues corvées récupère les minéraux précieux
que naguère, dans le ventre de leur jeunesse,
patiemment préparèrent des femmes rieuses.

(Les dames de Ninive
et autres préfectures d'avant-garde

## HAGIOS, ISCHYROS: SANCTUS, FORTIS
illusionist, conjuror,

child blowing hydrogen bubbles,

ovary laying galaxies in one menstrual cycle,

## DEUS SABAOTH: LORD OF THE ARMIES
Lord of the troops of the spirit,

Lord of our rout as well,

Lord too of our nights stretched toward death, toward life,

"Take me now," voices cried out in the night,

Lord of our first pause

in the joy of being alive,

in the shame of being alive

at the four corners of that stretched black sheet,

the sheet of the Requiem for so many absent bodies,

that empty sheet which we held: a private,

a sergeant, a captain, a major

holding by its four corners

that sheet hollowed by the invisible weight

of so many ashes left behind us.

At night in the tanks that rust on

the upper reaches of the Meuse, the spider weaves, the ant

on her long watch recovers the precious minerals

which once, in the womb of their youth,

laughing women patiently prepared.

(The ladies of Nineveh

and other prefectures of the avant-garde

ne savent pas ce qu'est l'amour du guerrier
pour le corps de ses frères. L'amour d'Achille
pour ce corps bien-aimé qu'Hector
abat dans la poussière, la fureur d'Achille
traînant dans la poussière les bras, les
boucles, les cuisses, douces aux femmes, d'Hector,
ce n'est pas désir désœuvré, ce n'est pas
vengeance de sérail, mais l'égoïste amour
par lequel le guerrier dans ce corps fraternel
d'avance pleure son propre corps, privé
de descendance, son corps avec lequel
périront des peuples non nés.)

Achille, qu'as-tu fait de ton frère Hector ?
L'ennemi aussi, cruel et pitoyable,
a perdu, par ta faute, son héritage,
l'ennemi aussi, a été jeté en pâture
aux idoles que tu n'as pas brisées.

L'évêque venu de Guéret dans la Creuse
parla en termes pénétrés et paternels et dit en substance
que ça nous apprendrait
à manquer les offices.
Et le drap vide
contenait par avance les cendres
de tous nos morts à venir :
Bernard, John,
Richard,
Maurice.

do not understand the warrior's love
for the body of his brothers. The love of Achilles
for that beloved body which Hector
brought down in the dust, the fury of Achilles
as he dragged through the dust the arms,
curls, thighs, dear to women, of Hector,
this is not deflected desire, this is not
settling scores in the seraglio, but the egotistical love
with which the warrior in this brother's body
weeps in advance for his own, deprived
of offspring, his body along with which
unborn peoples will perish.)

Achilles, what have you done with your brother Hector?
    The enemy too, cruel and pitiable,
        has lost his descendants by your doing.
    The enemy too, has been thrown as carrion
        to the idols that you did not shatter.


        The bishop come from Guéret in the Creuse valley
spoke paternally, penetratingly, said in substance
        that this would teach us
to miss church services.
                    And the empty sheet
            held in advance the ashes
        of all our dead to come:
            Bernard, John,
                Richard,
                    Maurice.

C'était une messe militaire : aux endroits
où d'ordinaire l'enfant de chœur agite sa sonnette, ici
éclataient les sauvages tambours,
bramaient les féroces clairons.
Ouvrez le ban !


Ombre de mon frère,
cendre de mon frère, qui fut homme,
c'est pour toi aussi qu'est dite la parole
la parole où l'on met genou en terre et
battent les prétoriens tambours :


ET HOMO FACTUS EST
Et fut fait
cendre, fut fait
peur, fut fait
pesanteur et ténèbre, fut fait
proie dans la gueule de la baleine, fut fait
doute, fut fait désespoir.


Seigneur des armées,
Seigneur des soldats,
Seigneur qui nous jeta dans la gueule de la baleine,
donne-nous aujourd'hui
non pas encore ta paix, mais
notre quotidienne nourriture d'erreur, de confusion,
d'aveuglement, d'injustice,
afin que, mâchant notre pain de poussière et de vent,

It was a military mass: whenever
a choirboy would have rung a bell, here
wild drums broke out,
fierce bugles wailed.
Begin the drumrolls!

Shadow of my brother,
ashes of my brother, who was a man,
it was also for you that the word was spoken
the word at which we go down on one knee and
the praetorian drumrolls sound:

ET HOMO FACTUS EST
And was made
ashes, was made
fear, was made
gravity and darkness, was made
prey in the whale's maw, was made
doubt, was made despair.

Lord of Armies,
Lord of soldiers,
Lord who threw us into the whale's maw,

give us today
not yet your peace, but
our daily nourishment of error, of confusion,
of blindness, of injustice,
so that, chewing our bread of dust and wind,

nous nous rappelions chaque jour
que l'Éternel n'est pas une poupée faite de main d'homme,
qu'Il n'est pas un fantôme docile à notre appel,
qu'Il ne donne, même contre Caïn, nulle victoire,
qu'Il n'est pas justice, pas ordre,
pas amour au sens de notre langage cannibale,
n'est pas vie, n'est pas dieu,
n'est rien de ce que dit une parole humaine.

Seigneur, donne-nous notre peine quotidienne
afin qu'elle soit pesée avec les cendres de nos frères.

Ombre,
que je ne vois pas, qui ne me parle pas,
que puis-je, sinon
dire que tu fus peur et courage,
amour et solitude,
homme que nous avons, si mal, aimé.

1954–55

we remember daily
that the Eternal is not a doll made by human hands,
that He is not a tame ghost who comes when we call,
that He grants no victory, not even over Cain,
that He is not justice and not order,
not love as our cannibal language defines it,
is not life, is not god,
is nothing that can be uttered in a human word.

Lord, give us this day our daily sorrow
so that it can be weighed with our brothers' ashes.

Shadow
whom I do not see, who does not speak to me
what can I do, besides
say that you were fear and courage,
love and solitude,
man that we, so inadequately, loved.

## PSAUME

La baleine, dit Jonas, c'est la guerre et son black-out.
La baleine, c'est la ville et ses puits profonds et ses casernes
La baleine, c'est la campagne et son enlisement dans la terre et l'épicerie
      et la main morte et le cul mal lavé et l'argent,
La baleine, c'est la société, et ses tabous, et sa vanité, et son ignorance.
La baleine, c'est (dans bien des cas, mes frères, mes sœurs) le mariage.
La baleine, c'est l'amour de soi. Et d'autres choses encore que je vous dirai
Plus tard quand vous serez un peu moins obtus (à partir de la page x).
La baleine, c'est la vie incarnée.
La baleine, c'est la création, en fin de compte superflue, mais indispensable
  pour cette expérience
      gratuite et d'ailleurs quasiment inintelligible.
La baleine est toujours plus loin, plus vaste ; croyez-moi, on n'échappe guère,
  on échappe difficilement,
      à la baleine.
La baleine est nécessaire.

Et ne croyez pas que vous allez tout comprendre comme cela d'un coup.

     Car enfin,
     Bien sûr la guerre est emmerdante
     Bien sûr la société
     Bien sûr le mariage
        Mais on n'a pas encore trouvé d'autre école

## PSALM

The whale, says Jonah, is war and its blackouts.
The whale is the city and its deep wells and its barracks.
The whale is the country stuck in its mud and its one grocery
        and the pulled punches and the unwashed crotches and the money.
The whale is society, and its taboos, its vanity, its ignorance.
The whale is (in so many cases, my brothers, my sisters) marriage.
The whale is self-love. And still other things that I'll tell you
Later, when you are a bit less obtuse (after page x).
The whale is incarnate life.
The whale is creation, superfluous after all is said and done, but indispensable
    for that
        gratuitous and after all almost incomprehensible experiment.
The whale is always farther, vaster; believe me, you barely escape, you have
    a hard
        time escaping from the whale.
The whale is necessary.

And don't think that you'll understand everything all in one go.

            Because after all,
            Of course war is a bloody bore
            Of course society
            Of course marriage
                But we haven't yet found a better way

De sorte qu'en fin de compte
Il ne reste en dernière analyse, comme cause d'emmerdement
Que l'amour de soi-même.
Car il faut savoir : l'on regarde au-dedans ou au-dehors
(Comme moi quand elle ouvrit la bouche — ou à travers moi).
Ainsi justement : la guerre,
La société, le mariage... il y en
A qui se servent comme
De tremplin pour sauter plus loin qu'eux-mêmes...

So that in the end

In the last analysis, all that's left as the source of bloody boredom

Is self-love.

For you must know, looking within or without

(As I did when the whale opened its jaws — or through me).

That precisely: war,

Society, marriage . . . there are those

Who make use of them

As a springboard to leap beyond themselves . . .

## CANTIQUE DE JONAS

Nous avons passé l'âge de nous plaindre ;
De quoi au fait nous plaindrions-nous ?
Il y a beau temps qu'on est sevré de la baleine maternelle.
Nous avons été dans la gueule de la baleine guerre
Et elle nous a recrachés sur le rivage.
Geignards ou glorieux, nous avons passé l'âge.

Moi, dit Jonas, à la fin d'une phrase je mets un point.
Et les majuscules au début de chaque ligne c'est uniquement parce que
Ça fait plus joli à l'œil, chaque imprimeur vous dira ça.
Évidemment pour celui qui écoute un autre lui lire ce n'est pas pareil
Et lui ça lui est égal qu'il y ait des majuscules.
Pourtant, Seigneur — et certes, ce que j'en dis,
Ce n'est pas pour élever ma voix contre l'Éternel.
Plutôt contre moi et pour remâcher ma folie
Dont le goût dans ma bouche qui s'édente est amer.
Contre ma folie et contre ce vide de moi
Qui de moi-même fait comme
Une baleine de vanité, une baudruche de vent.

Mais en l'absence du Seigneur je m'assieds et m'attriste.

De quoi pourtant, de quoi Jonas se plaindrait-il ?
Je suis vivant, dit Jonas, pas très vivant

## CANTICLE OF JONAH

We've gotten too old for complaining;
What, after all, would we complain about?
It's been a long time since we were weaned from the whale Mother.
We were in the maw of the whale War
Who spit us back onto the shore.
Whiners or heroes, we're past the age for it.

As for me, says Jonah, I put a period at the end of a sentence.
And the capital letters at the beginning of each line are only because
It looks better, any printer will tell you that.
Of course, when someone listens to someone else reading it isn't the same
And it doesn't matter to him if there are capital letters.
However, Lord—and of course, what I have to say
Is not to raise my voice against the Almighty.
Rather against myself and to brood over my own folly
Whose taste in my mouth as it loses its teeth is bitter.
Against my madness and against this emptied self
Which makes of myself something like
A whale of vanity, a wind-filled balloon.

But in the Lord's absence I sit down and sorrow.

Of what, though, of what would Jonah complain?
I am alive, says Jonah, not very alive

Puisque l'Esprit si rarement si brièvement me visite
Mais je suis vivant la bouche encore pleine
De mer et des humeurs âcres de la bête
Et pas très remis encore du mal de mer
Mais au total il n'y a pas à dire ça va
Et quand ça ne va pas, on fait aller.

Palmes, dans le ciel vert des oiseaux de passage
Au bord de l'eau, le soir encore brûlant
Échoué sur la côte du Brésil j'ai levé les yeux
et remercie l'Éternel qui me tient dans le creux de sa main.

Ce n'est pas tellement que je m'accuse
Ni d'ailleurs que j'essaie de me justifier.
Quoi ! J'ai peu menti, jamais tué en fait et
Presque jamais en pensée ; pour le reste, c'est entendu,
Flemmard et peloteur et parfois geignard
Personne au total de particulièrement, de bien intéressant.
Ô liquéfaction métaphysique, noyade bouddhique
Ô dispense de composer une personne superflue
Ô lassitude et secret désir d'enfin se perdre pour de bon
Dans les ténèbres internes de quelque baleine définitive.

Sentinelle, dis-nous la fin de la nuit.

Bonne affaire, bon aloi, bonnes fortunes
Bon usage de mon bon droit,
Bon air, bonne à tout faire, bon enfant,

Since the Spirit visits me so seldom.
But I am alive my mouth still full
Of sea and the beast's acrid secretions
And not yet entirely done with seasickness
But all in all there's nothing to say things are going right
And when they don't go right we make them go.

Palm fronds, migratory birds in the green sky
At the water's edge, dusk light still burning
Washed up on the Brazilian shore I raised my eyes
And thanked the Almighty who holds me in his hand's hollow.

It's not so much that I accuse myself
Nor for that matter try to justify myself.
Why? I didn't lie much, never killed in fact and
Hardly ever in thought; for the rest, granted, I
Was an idler, a lecher, sometimes a whiner
All in all no one particularly interesting.
O metaphysical liquefaction, Buddhist drowning
O exemption from composing a superfluous person
O lassitude and secret wish to lose oneself once and for all
In the internal darkness of some definitive whale.

Watchman, what of the night?

Good deal, good quality, good luck
Good use of my goodwill,
Well made, maid of all work, good-natured,

Bonne vie, bonne à rien faire,
Quand ça ne va pas, on fait aller.
Ah l'époque est intéressante, notez bien
ah, le moi est intéressant
mais celui qui est établi, celui qui vit dans l'entre-deux
celui qui n'aime assez ni son Moi ni Dieu
celui qui a été craché des ténèbres de la baleine personnelle
sur un rivage vide où il n'a pas su parler à Dieu
celui-là, que fera-t-il ?

Good life, made of no work, good for nothing,
When things don't go right we make them go.
Oh, how interesting these times, take note,
oh, how interesting the self
but the one who is settled, the one who lives in the intervals,
the one who loves neither his Self nor his God enough
the one spat out from the darkness of his personal whale
onto an empty shore where he did not know how to speak to God
that one, what will he do?

Rouge dans la brume

# Red in the Fog

C'était dimanche. J'étais venu, sans prévenir,
Sur ce qui semblait l'appel d'une lettre affectueuse et tendre,
par le train de nuit, 3e classe, billet militaire,
de Paris à Strasbourg.
                    Elle n'est pas là.
Partie en auto, la veille.
                    Bon.
J'ai lu. Je suis allé déjeuner à son restaurant habituel. Pas vue.
Je suis rentré. J'ai lu. Dans je ne sais plus quel
Écrit ô si éminemment critique, si
Sérieusement viril de M. de M. (qui a toujours eu
L'énorme mérite de citer la plupart de ses sources)
L'ange de silence a fait devant moi lever
Comme la colombe qui vient dire à Noé qu'il est sauvé des eaux
(de l'amertume ; eaux de l'amertume)
La phrase qui pendant ce long voyage m'a tenu lieu
de précepteur, d'ange gardien (quand le mien était occupé ailleurs),
de règle :
            «Je, note Pascal,
            ne suis la fin de personne
            et n'ai pas de quoi vous satisfaire.»
Pourtant,
            ma pente naturelle, par vantardise
            moscovite, par mollesse alémanique,

# IT WAS SUNDAY . . .

It was Sunday. I had come, unannounced,
Invited by what seemed an affectionate, tender letter,
On the night train, third class, military ticket,
From Paris to Strasbourg.

                She wasn't there.
Had left, in a car, the previous evening.

                Well then.
I read. I went to have lunch in her usual restaurant. Hadn't seen her.
I came back. I read. In I no longer know which
Essay oh so eminently critical, so
Seriously virile by M. de M. (who has always had
The enormous merit of citing most of his sources)
The angel of silence held up before me
Like the dove who comes to tell Noah that he is saved from the waters
(of bitterness; waters of bitterness)
The sentence that, during the long journey, had served me
As a tutor, as a guardian angel (when mine was otherwise occupied),
As a rule:

                "'I,' Pascal notes,
                'am no one's purpose
                and do not have the means to satisfy you.'"

And yet

                my natural inclination, out of Muscovite
                boastfulness, out of Germanic spinelessness,

par toute ma tripe stupide

ma pente est de faire plaisir.

Et parfois, Dieu sait,

j'ai perdu 10 ans de ma vie (11 ans)

pour faire plaisir, i. e. pour faire le

grand Seigneur

(l'orange achetée en cachette)

j'ai payé, tant mal que bien,

— te souvient-il du jour de ce

Grand brouillard

On allait enfin pouvoir fuir sans adresse,

Les remorqueurs sur le fleuve invisible

mugissaient comme des vaches sous l'orage,

un orage d'invisibilité,

un orage dans nos cœurs (pas le tien ?)

un orage dans notre sang

le brouillard se leva.

Trop tard.

Au coin de la rue je rencontrai Mr. Eliot qui lui aussi

attendait l'autobus.

How pleasant to meet Mr. Eliot quand on a du moins

la bonne fortune d'être un autre, de n'avoir pas du moins

à subir les emmerdements qui pour Mr. Eliot

déroulent fatalement de sa nécessité

d'être lui-même Mr. Eliot.

Je n'ai pas de quoi vous satisfaire.

Or, il se trouve

Que j'ai toujours trouvé tant mal que bien de quoi

down to my stupid core

my inclination is to please.

And there were times, God knows,

I've lost 10 years of my life (11 years)

trying to please, i.e., playing the

grand Seigneur

(the orange bought in secret)

I paid, for worse or better

—do you remember the day of the

Thick fog

We'd at last be able to run away, with no address,

The tugboats on the invisible river

mooed like cows in the storm,

a storm of invisibility,

a storm in our hearts (but not yours?),

a storm in our blood

the fog lifted.

Too late.

At the street corner I met Mr. Eliot, who was also

waiting for the bus.

How pleasant to meet Mr. Eliot when at least one has

the good luck to be someone else, to not, at least,

put up with the bloody hassle that for Mr. Eliot,

follows fatally from the necessity

of being himself Mr. Eliot.

I do not have the means to satisfy you.

And yet it seems

that I always found for worse or better what would

à peu près satisfaire,
tous ces autres, celle qui mendiait, celle qui proposait
au passant d'aller dans sa cuisine ouvrir l'armoire
pour y goûter ces délicieuses et par elle accumulées longuement
délicieuses confitures de néant, celle
qui avait envie d'un jouet, celle
— assez ! — j'ai eu de quoi.
Je n'ai pas eu, pour toi seule,
ma choisie, ma pour moi et non par moi choisie,
ma bien-aimée,
                    mon avarement aimée,
(celui qui, ayant distribué son bien,
    il n'a plus qu'un morceau de pain
    et un reste d'eau, dira-t-on qu'il est
    avare. — Oui, on le dira, avec raison.)
On le dira avare avec raison. Il n'avait qu'à
Garder un peu de son bien.
                    Pour toi seule,
ô de toute façon trop tard présentement,
    trop tard,
            pour toi seule
je n'ai pas eu de quoi te satisfaire
        et présentement je n'aurai plus, — comment aurais-je ?
        tu n'es plus toi d'alors,
        je ne suis plus moi comme alors
        je n'aurai plus de quoi te satisfaire.
Laisse, après cela, laisse les remorqueurs,
    laisse-les, trapus et répugnants,

more or less satisfy
all those others, the girl who begged, the one who suggested
the passerby come into her kitchen, open the armoire
to taste those delicious, and stocked up there by her for a long time,
delicious preserves of nothingness, the one
who wanted a toy, the one
—enough!—I had the means.
I did not have, for you alone,
my chosen one, my for me and not by me chosen,
my beloved,
my avariciously loved
(the man who, having given away all he owns,
has only a crust of bread
and a drop of water, would one say that he was
a miser keeping them—Yes, one would say so, and rightly).
One would rightly say he was a miser. He had only to
Keep a little of what he owned.
For you alone,
oh in any case too late, at present,
too late,
for you alone
I did not have what would satisfy you
and presently I will no longer have—how would I?
and after all you are no longer you
and I am no longer I as I was then
I will no longer have the means to satisfy you.
Let them go, after all that, the tugboats,
let them go, squat and repulsive,

laisse-les, cul-de-jattes, fumeurs de cigares,
laisse-les gueuler dans les brumes désormais inutiles
je crache sur eux du haut du pont.
Bien entendu, il faut savoir ce que parler veut dire,
Je pourrais encore, demain, présentement,
même sans brouillard, et loin du fleuve,
dire : ça y est ! Partons !
mais non,
le brouillard bien sûr n'est pas ce visible brouillard
les remorqueurs sont d'excellents
remorqueurs où l'équipage est brave
et gagne sa vie petitement débonnaire.
Je ne suis la fin de personne et n'ai pas de quoi vous satisfaire.
Oh, à poil ! crierai-je, comme au collège et au régiment,
à poil les dames d'une certaine élévation de sentiments
à poil les dames qui savent arranger leur vie et même en plus être de bon
    conseil
qu'on les donne à foutre aux mendiants.
Brouillard
brouillard
brouillard sur ta prévision, ta volonté.
Bonjour, trop tard bonjour,
bonjour mon cœur ta place par avance
est incontestablement sans hypothèque,
oh nous ne pourrons pas bâtir
certes, nous avons planté
mais nous ne pourrons pas
nous asseoir à l'ombre de cet arbre unique.

let them go, legless, cigar smokers,
let them squall in the fog, useless from now on,
I spit on them from the bridge.
Of course, one needs to know what one means,
I might still, tomorrow, presently,
even with no fog, and far from the river,
say, That's it! Let's go!
but no,
the fog was not, of course, this visible fog
the tugboats are excellent
tugboats whose crews are brave
easygoing and just getting by.
I am no one's purpose and do not have the means to satisfy you.
Oh, strip them naked!, I'll cry, the way we did in grade school and in the army,
strip those ladies with their finer feelings
strip those ladies who know how to manage their lives and on top of that give
good advice
and let the beggars fuck them.
Fog
fog
fog on your expectations, on your desires.
Good day, too late good day,
good day, my heart, your place is incontestably
and in advance secured
oh we cannot build
yes of course we planted
but we will not be able
to sit in the shadow of that only tree.

bontard cœurjour,
bon cœur, tardjour,
je me souviens
du soir d'été,
allant faire nos emplettes
le long du cimetière de tous les cimetières parisiens l'un des
moins infectés de musiciens de second
ordre et de visiteuses à règles
douloureuses,
nous allions faire nos emplettes chez les commerçants du quartier...

Goodlate, dayheart
good heart, lateday
I remember
a summer evening
on the way to do our shopping
alongside the one cemetery of all Paris cemeteries
least infested with second-class musicians
and women mourners
with menstrual cramps,
we went to do our shopping in the neighborhood . . .

rouge dans la brume le cœur de l'insensé
comme une boîte aux lettres avale de faux espoirs
s'arrête comme un bus aux arrêts facultatifs
ô cœur à deux étages ô cœur où la prochaine levée sera demain
ah si les attachés avaient mieux potachés
ils mettraient en alexandrins
du Times sibyllin les éditos bicéphalins

pour un chantecler sortant de chez sa philomèle
parfois un philomel sort de chez son aiglonne
où si toujours léda ariane médée toujours abandonnées
toujours de quelle faim blessées est-ce depuis toujours
qu'elles sont daphnées captives par les racines
oh il faudrait récrire les métamorphoses
on pourrait dire des tas de si pénétrantes choses
oh il y aurait à déployer tout un néosymbolisme
si revigorant pour le métabolisme
oh même les plus couturières des ambassadrices
soudain se reprendraient à vibrer de la matrice

au coin de la rue, d'après quel chêne nain nommée,
au coin du bistro qui fait le coin après le droguiste
qu'il est agréable de rencontrer Mister Eliot
Il n'a rien à dire d'ailleurs, on le comprend, sinon

## RED IN THE FOG . . .

red in the fog the neurotic's heart
swallows false hopes like a letterbox
stops like a bus at all the request stops
O double-decker heart, heart whose next collection time is tomorrow
ah, if the managers had done their homework
they would have set in meter and with rhymes
the bicephalous leaders of the *Times*

for a chanticleer leaving his nightingale's nest
or even a nightingale leaving his eaglette's eyrie
where if leda ariadne medea are always abandoned
always wounded by what hunger have they been
always daphnes held captive by their roots
oh the metamorphoses should be rewritten
such a load of such shrewd stuff could be said
and such a necessary neosymbolism
would reinvigorate the metabolism
the most dressmakerly ambassadress
would feel vibrations in her uterus

at the corner of a street named for what dwarf tree,
in a corner of the corner bistro beside the hardware store
how pleasant to meet Mr. Eliot
Moreover he clearly has nothing to say besides

qu'il fait beau ne fait-il pas, ou moins beau que la veille
d'ailleurs qu'y aurait-il à dire, en vérité, qu'y a-t-il
à dire jamais il y a peu à dire il n'y a qu'à attendre
et en attendant tant mal que bien on s'occupe
avec tout compte fait peu de profit pour quiconque
voilà ce que pourrait vous dire cet homme intègre
ce joueur de quilles qui n'a pas son pareil pour
avec grâce et précision abattre à chaque coup les
deux ou trois mêmes quilles et en vérité pourquoi
abattre tout un jeu de neuf il y a peu à dire
et si tout le monde avait le bon sens de se taire
un peu plus il n'y aurait rien à dire que les gens
n'auraient déjà par eux-mêmes pensé
le poète un jour peut-être, après des années
d'exercice, de discipline de la respiration,
de concentration sur l'idée mettons de la lettre a
dans le mot matches sur une boîte d'allumettes
après des années de solitude et quelques mois de
débauches et des stages sérieux dans des organismes
comme les eaux et forêts les pensions militaires
le poète chaque second, mettons chaque troisième jour
pendant cinq minutes, au coin de la rue, créera,
créera le sourire sur les lèvres du conductor de bus
créera un paysage mental dans la dame hépatique qui
passe créera un chant de remerciement qui s'élèvera
de l'hôtesse délaissée de l'air créera un chant
de louange chez ce jeune homme à melon bien né
un chant d'adoration des sept personnes qui attendent

that it's nice out, isn't it, or less nice than yesterday
moreover what is there to say, really, what is there
ever to say there isn't much to say one only has to wait
and waiting one occupies oneself as best one can
and when all is said and done at little advantage to anyone
that's what that upright man might say to you
that bowler who has no match at
knocking down with precision and grace the
same two or three skittles and really why
knock down all nine at once there isn't much to say
and if everyone had the good sense to be silent
more often there would be nothing to say that people
had not thought themselves already
perhaps the poet one day, after years
of exercise, of controlled breathing,
of concentration on the idea, let's say, of the letter *a*
in the word *matches* on a matchbox
after years of solitude and a few months of
debauchery and internships in organizations like
the Ministry of Agriculture, Water, and Forests, or Military Pensions
the poet, every second, or let's say every third day
for five minutes, at the street corner, will create,
create a smile on the bus conductor's lips
create a mental landscape within the liverish lady
passing by create a song of thanks which will rise
from the jilted airline hostess, create a song
of praise from that well-born young man in a bowler hat
a song of adoration from the seven people waiting

le bus le poète dans les grandes occasions nationales
sera chargé sur liste civile de la maison du roi
ou de la reine le matin du solstice d'été, dans
le quart d'heure qui suit l'aube, de mentalement
diffuser sur toutes les ondes courtes utilisées
par convention internationale par la communauté
londonienne et des home-counties, de diffuser
un cantique d'allégresse et de contentement les poètes
ne pourront plus se plaindre de la crise sociale et
des innovations fâcheuses de physiciens qui pourtant
n'ont très exactement rien fait d'autre que les poètes
à savoir de faire joujou, ne pourra plus se plaindre
de l'inégalité des salaires de l'absentéisme au culte
de la confusion du langage le poète conformément à sa
demande expresse sera enfin réintégré de plein
fonctionnement dans la société, aveugle par
décision prénatale, ou sourd, selon les besoins
annuellement prévus en poètes lyriques ou descriptifs
visuels ou auditifs, le poète aura fini de rigoler
ou de geindre à spender l'âme tout ça vous pend au nez
heureusement, je dis heureusement il y aura on verra
les débuts de la floraison de l'école de tombouctou
néomatérialiste néorationnelle en ce sens précis
qu'on aura découvert que l'esprit invisible est
matière seule efficace seule subtile et que la raison
consiste à se rendre compte que la moindre des
opérations de Dieu n'a strictement aucun rapport avec
une opération intellectuelle ah je prévois les

for the bus the poet on great national occasions
will be charged on the king's official list
or the queen's on the morning of the summer solstice,
in the fifteen minutes following the dawn, to
mentally broadcast on all the short waves used
by international agreement by the London
community and the Home Counties, to broadcast
his canticle of contentment and joy poets
will no longer complain about the social crisis and
the regrettable innovations of physicists who nonetheless
have precisely nothing to do but just what poets do
play with toys, no longer complain
about unequal salaries sparse church attendance
the disorder of language the poet in accordance with his
formal request will be finally reintegrated
into full participation in society, blind by prenatal
decision, or deaf, according to the annually
predicted needs for lyric or descriptive, visual
or auditive poets, the poet will be done with joking
or moaning to Spender the soul he had it coming
happily, I say happily there will be you'll see
the nascent flowering of the school of timbuktu
neomaterialist neorational in the specific sense
of having discovered that the invisible spirit is
matter, the only efficient, the only subtle matter and that reason
consists in realizing that the slightest of God's
acts has absolutely no relation to
an intellectual action oh I can foresee the

beaux préludes pour orgue verbal la place retrouvée
du hasard grâce aux accidents de la machine les
registres savamment poussés tirés pour obtenir à
l'improviste la basse de la mélancholie monophysite
les fraîches verdures les timbres clairs de l'espoir
les jaunes sereins de l'ironie sans rancune sur les
pédales répétant l'accord solitude union
le poète n'aura plus qu'à bien se tenir puisqu'à
la moindre dissonance interdite on verra sursauter
la courbe statistique de l'aliénation mentale ou
de la séparation de biens alors que les virtuoses
de même abaisseront la fréquence des accidents
maritimes de l'anémie des malentendus
parlementaires et qu'il sera réservé aux grands
talents qu'on reconnaîtra le génie poétique au
seul fait d'avoir opéré une chute soudaine dans
le graphique du cancer et de la maladie du sommeil
la maladie mécanique du sommeil qui se communique
par stylos somnoactifs par téléphones somnophiles
grande époque l'école de tombouctou au lieu
des époques geignardes où comme sous louis soleil
ou péricles tous les vieillards se plaignent de
la confusion des valeurs on verra les contraventions
sous forme d'insomnie de deux heures le temps de
réapprendre à reprendre son souffle le vol puni
par une semaine d'obligation d'accepter des
cadeaux utiles, l'avarice par un mois d'irrésistible
générosité la cruauté par une année de masochisme —

lovely preludes for verbal organ the rediscovered
role for chance thanks to mechanical accidents the
organ's stops expertly pushed pulled out to obtain
the unexpected bass of monophysite melancholy
the fresh greens in the clear hope tones
the serene yellows of ungrudging irony on the
pedals repeating the chord solitude union
but the poet will have to watch out because at
the slightest forbidden dissonance there'll be a jump
in the statistical curve of mental illness or
marital separations whereas these virtuosos
will nonetheless lower the rates of maritime
accidents anemia parliamentary
misunderstandings and the great talent
of poetic geniuses will be recognized by
the fact of their having caused a sudden drop
on the graphs of cancer and of sleeping sickness
the mechanical sleeping sickness transmitted
by somnoactive pens and somnophilic telephones
the great era of the school of timbuktu instead
of those whingeing epochs when under louis the sun king
or pericles all the old geezers complained
about the confusion of values you'll see traffic tickets
in the form of two hours of insomnia the time
to learn to catch your breath theft punished
by a week of being obliged to accept
useful gifts, avarice by a month of irresistible
generosity cruelty by a year of masochism —

non, par une année d'emprisonnement dans l'écorce
d'un arbre, — grande époque, les premiers
barrages mentaux pour l'accumulation du pouvoir
divinatoire les premiers transports en commun
d'énergie physiologique, les premières routes à
grande communication transcollectives d'énergie
spirituelle élémentaire, de quoi pour la ménagère
et le retraité réussir sans peine de petites opérations
simples de transfert de menus objets, ou de
nettoyage affectif des appartements. La punition pour
les élèves paresseux consistera à traduire vingt lignes
d'obscurophilie 20ᵉ s. en alexandrins hugoliens
exemples ad lib : sorti de madelon je prends la
mitraillette — horreur un e non compté à la césure...

no, by a year of imprisonment in the bark
of a tree—a great era, the first
mental dams to collect divinatory
power, the first public transports
of physiological energy, the first
transcollective highways of rudimentary
spiritual energy, so that the housewife
and the retiree can easily accomplish
the teleportation of small objects, or
emotional housecleaning. The punishment
for lazy pupils will be translating twenty lines
of twentieth-century obscurophilia into hugolian
alexandrines: examples ad lib: pulled out of madelon
I grabbed a tommy-gun—horrors an uncounted *e* at the caesura . . .

## LES PONTS DE BUDAPEST

Ils m'ont pendu pour avoir voulu vivre.
Ils m'ont pendu pour n'avoir pas tué.
Ils — ce ne sont pas les mêmes tous les jours — m'ont pendu
pour avoir cru ce que prédisent les autres
dans leurs livres d'école du soir pour adultes arriérés. Ils m'ont pendu
pour rien. Pour oublier la peur. Pour étrangler la honte.

Écoute, sur les ponts de Budapest, coexister
les pendus de tous catéchismes, de toutes cosmogonies.
Une fois le mauvais moment passé, on se tient compagnie
plus on est de pendus, plus on peut causer
au point où l'on en est, plus on peut rire.
Le vent du beau Danube bleu remplit nos poches à jamais vides de grenades
le givre raidit les défroques de nos corps. Six jours durant
j'ai trimé dur ; le septième jour je me suis reposé, j'ai vu.

D'étranges mandragores vont naître sur les routes
quand les chars, quand les chiens, quand les égouts en débordant
auront disséminé dans toutes les veines de la terre, dans toutes
ses matrices ce foutre de pendus, ce sang
giclant en pluie équatoriale sur les arbres gluants
ces lambeaux de muqueuses et d'os et d'ongles de gamines de treize ans
pour de précoces noces habillées de grenades
se glissant sous les chars pour se faire avec eux sauter.

## THE BRIDGES OF BUDAPEST

They hanged me for having wanted to live.
They hanged me for not having killed.
They—it's not the same ones every day—hanged me
for having believed what the others foretold
in their textbooks at the night school for retarded adults. They hanged me
for nothing. To forget their fear. To strangle their shame.

Hear them, on the bridges of Budapest, coexist,
the hanged men of every catechism and cosmogony.
Once the bad moment is over, we keep each other company,
the more hanged men there are, the more conversation,
where we're at now, we can laugh all the more.
The wind on the blue Danube fills our pockets now emptied forever of grenades,
frost stiffens our cast-off bodies. For six days
I slaved away; the seventh day I rested, I saw.

Strange mandrakes will be born on the roads
when the tanks, when the dogs, when the overflowing sewers
will have spread into all the veins of the earth, into all
its wombs this jism of hanged men, this blood
spurting in equatorial rain on the slimy trees
these scraps of membrane and bone and nail of thirteen-year-old girls
for precocious weddings bedecked in grenades
slipping under the tanks to blow themselves up with them.

Contre, dans la grande balance stupide — contre
le plateau où s'entassent les mots qui ne veulent rien dire et tout dire
les mots qui ne font pas de pain, les mots qui ne font pas l'amour,
les mots faits de vent recueilli dans les barbes depuis longtemps pourries
de professeurs à caleçons longs pour révolutions en pantoufles,
contre les mots qui tuent sans voir, sans regarder quiconque,
contre les gens qui vivent d'empêcher de vivre,
contre les gens qui soixante ans durant se vengent de leurs tristes enfances,
contre : des garçons livreurs, des ferblantiers, des vidangeurs,
des typographes, des laitiers, de petits télégraphistes,
quelques gamines de treize, douze, dix ans
soudain pubères quand il s'agit de se glisser, pour l'étrangler,
dans l'alcôve de métal et de feu du boucher.

Nous avons arrosé, labouré, ensemencé les esplanades,
nous avons sur l'asphalte passé la herse et la houe,
nous avons moissonné. À toi, Ivan, de faire la vendange !
Ivan, ô fils de truie, ô fils de femme chrétienne,
enfant de goret, enfant de bagnard sibérien, Ivan aux mille visages,
Ivan d'une seule misère, c'est contre toi, c'est avec toi,
c'est à côté de toi, c'est aussi pour toi que je me suis battu
contre ton frère Ivan, contre mon frère Janos.
Le vent nous fait valser au même lampadaire.
Du plus haut bec de gaz, ohé Janos, toi qui nous pètes sur la tête
vois-tu venir les chars américains ? vois-tu descendre en parachute
les volontaires titistes, progressistes, libertaires, humanistes ?
T'as voulu faire le fier, Janos. Pas comme nous

Against, in the great stupid scale—against
the platter where words pile up that mean nothing and everything,
the words that don't make bread, the words that don't make love,
the words made of wind gathered from the long-rotten beards
of professors dressed in long johns for a revolution in slippers,
against the words which kill without seeing, without looking at anyone,
against the people who live by keeping others from living,
against the people who revenge themselves sixty long years for their sad childhoods,
against: delivery boys, ironmongers, cesspool emptiers,
typographers, milkmen, little telegraph boys,
a few girls thirteen, twelve, ten years old
suddenly pubescent when it's a question of slipping, to strangle him,
into the butcher's alcove of metal and fire.

We watered, plowed, seeded the esplanades,
over the asphalt we passed the harrow and the hoe,
we reaped. Your turn, Ivan, to harvest!
Ivan, O son of a sow, O son of a Christian woman,
child of a piglet, child of a Siberian convict, Ivan of a thousand faces,
Ivan of a single poverty, it's against you, it's with you,
it's beside you, it's also for you I fought
against your brother Ivan, against my brother Janos.
The wind makes us waltz on the same lamppost.
From the highest gas lamp, ohé, Janos, you who fart on our heads,
do you see the American tanks coming? do you see them descend
with parachutes, the Titoist, progressive, libertarian, humanist volunteers?
You wanted to play haughty, Janos. Not like us,

qui depuis tant d'années, dans tant de nuit, attendons,
dans tant de gel, dans tant de mort, attendons,
dans le toujours plus ridicule, plus nécessaire espoir, attendons,
quand nos gosses rentrés de l'école idolâtre prétendent nous apprendre
comment on fait un feu, un toit, un lit, un pain, comment
on tue le cochon (quand on en a un), comment le loup cherche pâture,
comment à chaque printemps le fleuve immensément fait craquer sa prison,
comment on vend ses légumes, comment on nourrit sa vieille mère,
comment on fait des enfants
comment on meurt.


Toi qui voulais un monde clair et fraternel, tu es servi,
toi qui toujours espères, sur ton peuple d'ivrognes et de fainéants
voir fondre une soudaine Pentecôte où tout le monde
s'embrassera en parlant russe parmi des pigeons de feu,
tu as réussi.
Autour des pendus danse la ronde des enfants perdus, dansent
les esprits des morts de massacres plus anciens. Forcément,
quand on donne une pareille fête, ça attire du monde, on fait recette
en attendant les sanglantes kermesses d'Ukraine, de Russie Blanche et
Baltique et Caucasienne et Turkestane et Sibérienne, voici des collègues
venus des petites fêtes de la famille humaine, répression de la Grande
Mutinerie, marche vers l'Ouest, village près de Tipiza liquidé à la bombe
l'année de la Libération, conquête du Congo, pacification de villages zoulous,
bantous, viets, malais, javanais, philippins, mandchous, mau-mau, tutti quanti.
Venez, collègues, faites comme chez vous.

who for so many years, in so much night, are waiting,
in so much ice, in so much death, waiting,
in ever more ridiculous and more necessary hope, waiting,
when our kids, come home from the idolatrous school, try to teach us
how to make a fire, a roof, bread, how
you slaughter the pig (when you have one), how the wolf seeks its food,
how every spring the river enormously shatters its prison,
how you sell your vegetables, how you feed your old mother,
how you make babies,
how you die.


You who wanted a frank and fraternal world, you've got it,
you who always hoped to see, on your people of drunkards and layabouts,
a sudden Pentecost pour down where everyone
would embrace speaking Russian among fiery doves,
you've succeeded.
Around the hanged men a circle of lost children dances, the spirits
of the dead in the most ancient massacres are dancing. Obviously
when you give a party like this it attracts people, you're a success,
while waiting for the bloody carnivals of Ukraine, White Russia,
Baltic, Caucasian, Turkestanian, Siberian, here are colleagues
come from the human family's little celebrations, suppression
of the Great Mutiny, march to the West, village near Tipiza liquidated by bombs
the year of the Liberation, conquest of the Congo, pacification of Zulu villages,
Bantu, Viet, Malaysian, Javanese, Philippine, Manchu, Mau Mau, tutti quanti.
Come, colleagues, make yourselves at home.

Tu parles bien, Ivan, tu as toujours aimé parler. Nous,
ici, maintenant, on a rentré cette récolte précise. On se repose,
on regarde. Et pour délirant, pour inutile que ça puisse être,
nous, ce qu'on a fait, maintenant, ici, tel quel,
ça nous plaît.

You speak well, Ivan, you always liked to talk. As for us,
here, now, we've brought in this particular harvest. We rest,
we have a look. And however outrageous, useless, it might be,
as for us, what we've done, here, now, as it is,
it pleases us.

## DÉPASSÉ. PROVISOIREMENT

Sombre. Mais l'espace plus vaste.
Moins de gens. Le sentier dans l'obscurité
mène-t-il vers une solitude plus vraie ?
Peut-être est-ce à cet âge, en ce lieu, ici
que se partagent les routes.

Sombres heures, journées, semaines. Ainsi
dans la plaine de ton enfance, les eaux très lisses,
très silencieuses. Et noires. Le cœur
s'est lassé de courir. À pas plus lents,
à pas presque égaux, ce cœur
nous entraîne sans bruit vers l'ampleur de la nuit.

Il ne désire plus. Ne gambade plus. Ne se cabre plus.
Mais à voix basse, dans la brise obscure, il chante encore.
Lente chanson linéaire, horizontale,
sans grincements, sans grimaces, sans cris.

Il est temps de dormir. Faut-il présentement
attendre le retour d'une aube plus mûre
pour un travail plus régulier ?
Ou faut-il déjà, faut-il vraiment, faut-il
descendre vers les rives de la grande eau souterraine ?

2/1/57

## OVERTAKEN. TEMPORARILY


Dark. But a wider space.
Less people. Does the path in the darkness
lead toward a more authentic solitude?
Perhaps it's at this age, in this place, here
that the roads divide.

Dark hours, days, weeks. Like this
on the plain of your childhood, the very smooth,
very silent waters. Black waters. The heart
has grown weary of running. With slower steps,
with almost measured steps, that heart
tugs us toward the fullness of night.

It no longer desires. No longer gambols. No longer rears up.
But with a low voice, in the dim breeze, still sings.
Slow, linear, horizontal song
with no creaking, no grimaces, no cries.

It's time to sleep. Must you, now,
await the return of a riper dawn
for a more steady job?
Or must you, must you really, must you
go down to the shore of the great underground waters?

Faut-il toujours attendre ?

Cancer — est-ce prévoir ?
Attendre ? remettre le jour de se rompre et se défaire.
Cancer, fausse adolescence, construction de mort
quand il faudrait laisser le vent jeter à bas
les dernières tuiles sur la poutre vermoulue.

Le jour où l'orage le frappe
   le vent de l'orage le guérit.
Le feu qui lui mordit le foie et les reins
   le guérit. Il faut mourir guéri.

Je serai nettoyé si
j'éclate au vent comme citrouille vieille.
Peut-être, pour un nouveau travail, ne reprend-on
que des objets bien nettoyés ?

Must there always be this waiting?

Cancer—is it anticipation?
Waiting? postpone the day of breaking and coming undone.
Cancer, false adolescence, construction of death
when the wind must be allowed to knock down
the last tiles on the worm-eaten roof beam.

The day when the storm strikes him
          the storm's wind cures him.
The fire that gnaws at his liver and loins
          cures him. He must die cured.

I would be cleansed if
I burst in the wind like an old pumpkin.
Perhaps, for new work, the only things taken
are those that were thoroughly cleansed?

PÂQUES 1957

1

Commence, recommence n'importe où !
Il importe désormais
seulement que tu fasses chaque jour
un quelconque travail, un travail
fait seulement avec attention, avec
honnêteté. Il importe seulement
que tu apportes à bâtir indéfiniment la réalité
(jamais finie) ta très très petite part quotidienne...
À travers la lunette ou par l'œil encore unique
tu vois lentement, en détail très mal,
au total assez bien. Assez pour t'orienter.
Assez pour savoir marcher, le chemin qui peu à peu
se découvre. Assez pour tant bien que mal
faire ta part. D'ailleurs, en fait,
importe-t-il, le détail du travail,
le détail des formes du pied dans le sable,
ou bien le but où tu finis, tard, assez las,
où tu finis peut-être, parfois, par arriver ?
Mais il n'y a pas de but non plus.
Le but recule toujours vers les sables non
atteints.

## EASTER 1957

### 1

Begin, begin again, no matter where!
From now on it only
matters that every day you do
some task, a task
performed attentively,
honestly. It only matters
that you add to the unending construction of reality
(never completed) your very small daily share . . .
Through glasses or with your remaining eye
you see slowly, rather badly in detail,
but all in all well enough. Well enough to get your bearings.
Well enough to follow the road that little by little
reveals itself. Well enough to do your part
as best you can. After all, in fact,
does it matter, the task's particulars,
the outline of the foot's form in the sand,
or the goal where you finish, late, tired enough,
where you finish perhaps, sometimes, by arriving?
But there is no goal either.
The goal is always receding toward the unreached
dunes.

## 2

Pâques est le contraire de Noël.
La place se vide, l'être disparaît.
C'est la fin de la vie visible et charnelle,
des repas, des heures de sommeil. C'est la fin
de l'action à la fois visible et douteuse, mesurable, mesurée,
tenue secrète, discrète.
            Seules deux, trois femmes rencontrent
le Présent. Elles ne se posent pas de questions, elles veulent
savoir ce qui est ou n'est pas. Puis quelques disciples, par groupes
y compris Thomas. Auquel il faut venir montrer.
Il y a ainsi des caractères, des esprit divers.
            En même temps, fleurs, arbres, vie qui déborde
les champs, animaux réveillés, activés à se joindre,
à nourrir, à tuer. Début de triomphe du visible, du
matériel, qui ne commencera à fondre, à disparaître
qu'au début de l'hiver. Splendeur des fourrures.
Splendeur des yeux, des pattes. Ignorance totale.
Ignorance du monde plus durable, plus long.
Est-ce le stade le plus gros, le plus lourd
de l'abêtissement visible pour l'âme, là où elle
ne peut même plus se souvenir, en tout cas plus dire...

## 3

Plus de somnifères. Plus d'apparences.
Plus de symboles, à vrai dire, ni pierres, ni plantes.
Ni maisons. Ni arbres.

## 2

Easter is the opposite of Christmas.
Space empties, the living being disappears.
It is the end of visible fleshly life,
of meals, of hours of sleep. It's the end
of action at once observed and dubious, measurable, measured,
kept secret, discreet.
       Only two or three women encounter
the Present. They don't ask themselves questions, they want
to know what is or isn't. Then a few disciples, in groups,
including Thomas. Who must be approached and shown.
Thus do characters, states of mind differ.
       At the same time, flowers, trees, life overflowing
the fields, awakened animals, moved to mate,
to feed, to kill. The triumph of the visible begins, the
material, which will not start to melt, to disappear
till the start of winter. Splendor of pelts.
Splendor of eyes, of paws. Total ignorance.
Ignorance of a more durable, longer-lasting world.
Is this the grossest, heaviest stage
of the stupefaction visible to the soul, there where it
cannot even remember, in any case no longer say . . .

## 3

No more sleeping pills. No more appearances.
No more symbols, in truth, neither stones nor plants.
Nor houses. Nor trees.

Venez sur mes sentiers déserts, avancez-vous
vers mes espaces déserts. Je serai désormais
la voix du silence, l'ombre à votre gauche les jours
de grande lumière, le son des pas sur les cailloux,
le temps qui passe et passe si lentement, si vite,
je suis votre silence et ce qui est autour, je suis
votre silence dans ce qu'il a rarement de plus profond.
Dites-moi bonsoir, dites-moi bonjour, bonjour surtout,
bonjour longtemps à l'orée des journées à travailler
dites-moi bonjour pour m'appeler moi maintenant,
moi à mon tour, toi à ton tour, nous à notre tour
pour nous appeler
à la *création*.

*Lundi, Pâques*

4

Écoute. Suis-moi. L'homme à la chapelle,
pardon, à l'église, anglicane, officielle, et tout,
expliquant, commentant, sans regarder personne
quelque parole fort brève de l'Épître aux Hébreux,
insiste sur cet enseignement central du Christ,
nous prédicant comme le plus grand de tous les pionniers.
Suis-moi. Viens à ma suite. Marche à ma suite.

Est-ce goût de la discipline ? de la modestie ?
est-ce intelligence et cœur véritables ?

Je ne sais pas. Je ne sais même pas
ce qui m'est dû, ce que je prends à injuste titre ?

Come forward on my deserted paths, approach
my deserted spaces. I will be henceforth
the voice of silence, the shadow at your left on days
of brilliant light, the sound of steps on pebbles,
time that passes and passes so slowly, so fast,
I am your silence and what surrounds it, I am
your silence and what's deepest, if seldom, in it.
Say goodnight to me, say good morning, good morning especially,
a long good morning as a workday starts
say good morning to me to call me, here and now,
me in my turn, you in your turn, us in our turn,
to call us
to the *creation*.

*Easter Monday*

4

Listen. Follow me. The man in the chapel,
excuse me, the church, Anglican, official and all that,
explaining, commenting on, while looking at no one,
some very brief word in the Epistle to the Hebrews,
insists on that essential teaching of Christ,
preaching to us like the greatest pioneer.
Follow me. Come along after me. Walk behind me.

Is it a predilection for discipline? For modesty?
Is it authentic intelligence and heart?

I don't know. I don't even know
what is due to me, what I take undeserving?

Je ne sais pas où je devrais m'arrêter.
Et téléphoner à ma conseillère ne me sert en vérité
à rien. À me rassurer vaguement, on peut dire tout au plus
quelques instants tout au plus. Ces oiseaux en fuite
emportent-ils un rayon, un bout, un minime
morceau de mon cœur ? Ou rien ? leur ombre ?
L'ombre de leur crainte et de leur légèreté ?
J'aurais ainsi beaucoup de questions à te poser.


5

Bec jaune, bec courbe, bec de lapin ou de
cygne. Ne m'apportent rien. Ne m'apprennent rien.
Il faut attendre. Dans le silence et le noir.
Dans l'ombre malsaine de la nuit tourmentée.
Dans le désordre. Il faut attendre sans même
un espoir précis. Il faut attendre jusqu'à ce que
le résultat attendu se soit réalisé.
C'est-à-dire attendre les moments, les chances,
les je ne sais quoi rarement réussis.
Adieu Floriane ! Je ne sais plus qui tu es,
à quoi, à qui tu ressembles. C'est trop loin.
C'est trop grêle, trop enfantin, trop inimportant,
trop libre de tout, simple caprice du cœur
ou est-ce de l'œil ? Les autres maintenant
voyagent, essayent bientôt de dormir. D'autres
se sont couchés et dorment profond. D'autres
lisent en un moment d'insomnie un dernier

I don't know when I ought to stop.
And telephoning my confidante would truthfully
be useless. She would vaguely reassure me, one might say at most,
for a few moments, at most. Those birds flying off,
are they carrying a ray, a crumb, a paltry
piece of my heart? Or nothing? their shadow?
The shadow of their fear and of their lightness?
I would have so many questions for you.


5

Yellow beak, curved beak, rabbit's nose,
swan's bill. Bring me nothing. Teach me nothing.
I must wait. In the silence and the dark.
In the tormented night's unsavory shadows.
In disorder. Must wait without even
a specific hope. Must wait until
the waited-for result has been achieved.
Wait, that is to say, for moments, opportunities,
the rarely fruitful I don't-quite-know-whats.
Farewell, Floriane! I no longer know who you are,
what or whom you resemble. It's too far.
It's too shrill, too childish, too unimportant,
too free of everything, only a whim of the heart,
or was it the eye? Right now the others
are traveling, will soon try to sleep. Still others
are in bed and sleeping deeply. And others,
insomniac, finish reading one last

chapitre. Dans d'autres longitudes, d'autres
célèbrent la dernière heure du jour ou la
première du matin. Le mistral ne règle rien.
Il faudra du temps pour faire une seule
observation simple et vraie.

*Lundi/mardi de Pâques, 01.20*

6

Saurais-je encore comment remplir le jour ?
Ou simplement comment attendre ?
Ne rien remplir ? N'y plus même penser ;
ne pas penser à distinguer entre
urnes pleines, urnes vides, mais seulement
entre celui qui dort, celui qui vraiment veille.

*02.30*

7

Qu'est-ce que c'est, quelle partie, quel non pas corps
mais quelle partie relative minime du corps, qu'est-ce que c'est
qui ne veut pas dormir ?

*04.15*

8

Attendre le matin, pourquoi ? Finira-t-il d'attendre ?
Permettra-t-il enfin d'aller dormir commodément ?
d'aller dormir profondément ? Comme si l'on était

chapter. In other longitudes, others
celebrate the last hour of the day or the first
hour of the morning. The mistral solves nothing.
It takes time to make a single
observation, simple and true.

*Easter Monday/Tuesday, 1:20 a.m.*

6

Would I still know how to fill a day?
Or simply how to wait?
Fill nothing? Not even think of it;
not think of how to tell the difference
between filled urns and empty urns, but only
between the sleeper and the one who truly keeps watch.

*2:30*

7

Which one is it, which part, which, not the body
but some comparatively minimal part of the body, which one is it
that doesn't want to sleep?

*4:15*

8

Wait for the morning, why? To be through with waiting?
Will it let me fall asleep comfortably at last?
To fall deeply asleep? As if I were

un être sain, établi dans sa santé aux heures usuelles.
Attendre le matin, qu'il vienne enfin poindre sur les
collines indifférentes, et répandre une lumière neuve
et toute fraîche sur les rues au reste indifférentes
parmi les spectateurs qui dorment.
Quand saurais-je revenir parmi les habitudes connues ?

*Mercredi 23, 01.45*

9

Qui a besoin de toi ? personne.
Y en aura sans doute qui ne détestent pas
prendre un verre, raconter une histoire, faire un tour,
causer, et qui en un sens, pour un moment,
si tu étais mort, regretteraient ta disparition.
Mais le fait qu'en fin de compte, pour toi, sur cette terre,
pas pour eux, tu sois disparu, ça ne changerait rien
à leur humeur, leur appétit, leur désir de bouger
et pourquoi cela changerait-il quoi que ce soit ?
Voici donc les limites à connaître clairement.
À l'intérieur de cette limite, il est quelque espace.
Rien de fou, mais assez pour l'homme vraiment
libre, vraiment raisonnable (en supposant que ce mot
ait un sens quelconque). Il s'agit, après tout
uniquement
de préparer le terrain généralement ingrat
sur lequel on va jeter le grain au demeurant médiocre
ou mieux encore : incertain, de ta difficile croissance.

a healthy being, affirmed in his health at habitual hours.
Wait for the morning, let it come at last and dawn
on the indifferent hills, spread new light,
all fresh, on the indifferent streets
among the sleeping spectators.
When will I be able to return to what I knew?

*Wednesday the 23rd, 1:45 a.m.*

9

Who needs you? No one.
Of course there are some who wouldn't mind
having a drink, telling a story, taking a walk,
just talking, and who, in a way, for a moment,
if you were dead, would regret your disappearance.
But the fact that in the end, for you, on this earth,
not for them, you've disappeared, wouldn't affect
their mood, their appetite, their wish to get going,
and why should that change anything at all?
Those, then, are the limits to keep in mind.
Within those limits, there's a bit of space.
Nothing outlandish, but enough for the really
free man, really reasonable (if that word still
means anything whatsoever). It's about, after all
only
preparing the usually ungrateful ground
where you will sow the seed, mediocre,
or, better still, uncertain, of your difficult growth.

Eux aussi, ils aiment dormir, ne rien faire de spécial,
croire un peu, lire beaucoup, se promener
et ne pas chaque jour être forcé à des choix inutiles
et inutilement spectaculaires. On ne veut pas que des choses
arrivent ; on veut qu'elles *soient* et ne changent que
lentement, très lentement, comme un tissu réel
sur un corps réel. Ceci dit, bien sûr
je remercie l'ange gardien et crois le reconnaître
pour autant que possible sans l'avoir encore *vu*.
Sans l'avoir même senti ou entendu ou même
réellement deviné. Mais je crois qu'il existe.
Comme le facteur après tout jamais vu
depuis six mois dans ce nouvel appartement.
Comme le temps va vite, avec ses dégâts
au moins aussi vite qu'avec ses plaisirs.
La petite à cette heure dort. Profonde, régulière
haleine. Profonde ? Peut-être, oui, et en tout cas
régulière. Un arbre peut-être croit sentir
des flairements d'insectes ou des animaux
se frottant le derrière contre ses épines,
ou des mouches cherchant le vol indéfini.
Cette écriture est devenue difficile, minuscule,
pas spécialement claire, et peut-être destinée
à retomber peut-être à un niveau confus,
peu propre. Il faut reprendre
en apprenant par des leçons élémentaires
concernant toute la longueur du corps.
Plus de force pour protéger dans le titre et les

And they, they also like to sleep, do nothing special,
believe a little, read a lot, take walks,
and not be forced each day to make useless
and uselessly spectacular choices. One doesn't want
things to happen; one wants them to *be*, and to only change
slowly, very slowly, like real tissue
of a real body. That said, of course
I thank the guardian angel and think I recognize him
as well as is possible without yet having *seen* him.
Without having felt or heard or even
really sensed him. But I believe he exists.
Like the postman whom after all I've never seen
after six months in this new apartment.
How quickly time goes with its damages
at least as quickly as with its pleasures.
My little daughter is sleeping at this hour. Deep, even
breaths. Deep? Perhaps, yes, and in any case,
even. A tree, perhaps, believes it feels
insects darting or animals scratching
their rump on its thorns
or flies in search of unlimited flight.
This writing has become hard to read, minuscule,
not terribly clear, and—perhaps—destined
to fall back—perhaps—to a confused
and dubious level. Better to start learning
again, with elementary lessons
concerning the whole length of the body.
No strength to protect the titles and credits

andouillettes le tirage de ton film ou qu'est-ce
et surtout ces dessins-couverture, avec tant
de dessins parfois déformés ou transformés en 2
par les couvertures à la « créateur».
Seigneur, permettez-moi
de garder patience, de ne pas demander trop,
de savoir attendre le non-prévisible,
le non-prévu, sorti brièvement de quelque
naufrage ou catastrophe, si l'on y échappe.

*Samedi 01.30*

## 10

rien à dire — tout à attendre
rien à assurer — tout à faire
rien à réclamer — tout à obtenir
d'ailleurs ce qu'est la poésie,
qui le sait, le sait vraiment ?
personne ne l' sait — personne ne l' fait
à coups sûrs, à coups sûrs dans la soupe,
dans la salade, dans le dessert.
Va te coucher et essaie dans ton sommeil
d'être.

*5/2/57, 01.15*

## 11

Voici refermée la porte qui menait
        aux eaux sombres et souterraines.

while developing your film, or is it
the cover drawing in particular, with so many
drawings sometimes deformed or cut in two
in "artistic" cover designs?
Lord, allow me
to stay patient, to not ask for too much,
to know how to wait for the unpredictable,
the unpredicted, emerged briefly from some
shipwreck or catastrophe, if we escape it.

*Saturday 1:30 a.m.*

## 10

nothing to say—everything to wait for
nothing to undertake—everything to do
Nothing to ask for—everything to gain
and anyway, what's poetry,
who knows, really knows?
no one knows it—no one does it
without a doubt, without a doubt in the soup,
in the salad, in the dessert.
Go to bed and try in your sleep
to be.

*5/2/57, 1:15 a.m.*

## 11

And there it is closed once more, the door that led
       to the dark, subterranean waters.

Certes, il y a encore du dégât. Un œil fermé,
Une ample cicatrice du crâne.
L'insomnie de la première partie de la nuit.
Les dents piteuses. La mémoire
encore médiocre. Mais tout ceci vivant.
Que fera-t-on désormais ?
Un travail sédentaire, un peu solitaire.
Un séjour principal à la campagne.
Que fera-t-on ? Ce qui demandera à être fait.
Ce qui se présentera. Ce qui
Insistera. Que fera-t-on ? On vivra.
Longtemps. Patiemment. Sans protestations.
On vivra parce qu'il faut vivre, parce qu'il faut
faire ce que l'on est né pour faire.
On ne cherchera plus à fuir. Il n'y a pas
de fuite possible, véritable. Il n'y a
que la possibilité de faire ce qu'on est né pour faire.

*5/3/57, 0100 heures*

## 12

Le désordre est tenace
le désordre toujours, dès que l'on cesse de vouloir
se rétablit de lui-même avec grande facilité.
Le désordre est-il la préparation de la mort
ou les biens au hasard de la vie,
non tonalisée, non ponctuée, non prévisible ?

Of course, there is still damage. One closed eye,
    A large scar on the skull.
The insomnia of the first part of the night.
    The wretched teeth. The still mediocre
memory. But all of that alive.
    What will you do from now on?
Sedentary work, somewhat solitary.
    A house in the country.
What will you do? That which must be done.
    That which presents itself. That which
insists. What will you do? You will live.
    A long time. Patiently. Without protesting.
You will live because you must live, because one must
    do what one was born to do.
You will no longer try to flee. There is no
    escape, no real one, possible. There is only
the possibility of doing what one was born to do.

*5/3/57, 0100 hours*

## 12

Disorder is stubborn,
Disorder, as soon as one has stopped wanting, always
returns by itself and easily.
Is disorder death's preparation
or life's goods acquired in passing,
untuned, unpunctuated, unpredictable?

Adieu sommeil, adieu vigueur !
l'esprit sans se lasser, sans se contenter
cherche sur les parois du cerveau éprouvé.
Le corps dort à demi, est gêné, fatigué,
ne réussit pas à s'opposer.
C'est agaçant, l'esprit n'apporte rien,
ne trouve rien, simplement cherche,
peut-être simplement bouge, mollement,
de quelques petits degrés de gauche à droite,
de droite à gauche, sans s'arrêter, sans se
contenter, sans se pacifier.
Cette morne veillée durera-t-elle longtemps ?

Farewell slumber, farewell energy!
The spirit, unwearied, unsatisfied,
scours the walls of the afflicted brain.
The body, half-asleep, is annoyed, tired,
doesn't manage to oppose it.
It's irritating, the spirit brings nothing,
finds nothing, only seeks,
perhaps only moves, sluggishly,
a few tiny degrees from left to right,
from right to left, without stopping, not
satisfied, finding no peace.
Will this dismal vigil go on for long?

JEAN-PAUL DE DADELSEN was born in Strasbourg, Alsace, in 1913. After teaching German literature in Marseille and Oran, he joined de Gaulle's Free French Army in London during World War II and was a correspondent for Albert Camus's newspaper *Combat*. He was a journalist for the BBC's French Service after the war. He began writing poetry seriously in his thirties and died of a brain tumor in 1957. Most of his work was published posthumously, notably, *Jonas* in 1962 and *Goethe in Alsace* (poems, essays, and recollections by friends) in 1982. His complete poems were published in the Poésie Gallimard series as *Jonas, suivi de Les Ponts de Budapest et autres poèmes*, in 2005.

MARILYN HACKER is the author of fourteen books of poems, including *Blazons* (2019), *A Stranger's Mirror* (2015), and *Names* (2010), and an essay collection, *Unauthorized Voices* (2010). Her sixteen volumes of translations of French and Francophone poets include Hédi Kaddour's *Treason* (2010), Vénus Khoury-Ghata's *A Handful of Blue Earth* (2017), Rachida Madani's *Tales of a Severed Head* (2012), and Emmanuel Moses's *Preludes and Fugues* (2016). She received the 2009 American PEN Award for poetry in translation for Marie Étienne's *King of a Hundred Horsemen*, the 2010 PEN Voelcker Award, and the international Argana Prize for Poetry from the Beit as-Sh'ir/House of Poetry in Morocco in 2011. She lives in Paris.